科技英语
阅读与实用英语写作

总主编　黄锦华
主　编　胡春华　刘甜甜
副主编　董月琳　王芳芳　韦艳梅
　　　　陈士芳　陆梅华　赵　丹
　　　　盛捷柯　邝江红　韦　俊
　　　　杜　卉　孙远用　宋琳琳
　　　　朱芬芬　李　敏

苏州大学出版社
Soochow University Press

图书在版编目(CIP)数据

科技英语阅读与实用英语写作/胡春华,刘甜甜主编. —苏州:苏州大学出版社,2016.6(2020.7重印)
ISBN 978-7-5672-1758-4

Ⅰ.①科… Ⅱ.①胡…②刘… Ⅲ.①科学技术—英语—阅读教学②科学技术—英语—写作 Ⅳ.①H31

中国版本图书馆 CIP 数据核字(2016)第 128689 号

书　　名:	科技英语阅读与实用英语写作
主　　编:	胡春华　刘甜甜
责任编辑:	金莉莉
封面设计:	刘　俊
出版发行:	苏州大学出版社(Soochow University Press)
地　　址:	苏州市十梓街1号　邮编:215006
印　　装:	苏州工业园区美柯乐制版印务有限责任公司
网　　址:	http://www.sudapress.com
E - mail:	yanghua@suda.edu.cn
邮购热线:	0512-67480030
销售热线:	0512-67481020
开　　本:	787mm×1092mm　1/16　印张:11　字数:247千
版　　次:	2016年6月第1版
印　　次:	2020年7月第6次修订印刷
书　　号:	ISBN 978-7-5672-1758-4
定　　价:	28.00元

凡购本社图书发现印装错误,请与本社联系调换。服务热线:0512-67481020

前　言

《科技英语阅读与实用英语写作》体现了教育部关于本科院校向应用技术型大学转型的指导意见，主要用于大学英语提高阶段的教学。旨在巩固并熟练应用在基础阶段所学的英语语言知识和阅读技能，拓宽语言知识面，扩大词汇量，同时提高对科技类英语文章的理解能力以及掌握常用应用文写作的技巧，为今后专业文献的阅读、科技信息的获取和常用应用文的书写打下良好的基础。

本书的阅读文章全部选自国内外原版科技书籍和网站，内容涉及汽车、机械、土木、电气与计算机、食品与化工、经济与管理等领域，选材广泛，信息量大，内容新颖，具有强烈的时代气息，体现了现代科技发展的成果和科技英语的特点。

本书由多年从事大学英语教学和科技英语教学的一线教师精心设计和编写。全书分为三个部分：第一部分为阅读基础篇，共4个单元；第二部分为阅读专业篇，共7个单元；第三部分为应用文写作。每个单元分 Text A 和 Text B。应用文写作部分分6个单元进行讲解：说明书、简历、通知、常用信函、摘要以及参考文献。

全书语言规范，篇幅适中，语言难度略高于大学英语四级阅读。每单元的练习都提供了参考答案及解析。本书附录附有常见院系名称双语对照、常见大学专业学科双语对照、常见专业技术职称名称双语对照和常见公司企业各部门名称双语对照。另外，还有生词表供学生学习。

在编写过程中，编者参阅了国内外大量的期刊以及其他各种材料，在此向提供材料的各位同仁表示感谢。由于时间仓促，编者水平有限，遗漏、错误之处在所难免，望各位同仁和读者不吝指正。

编　者

2016年5月

阅读基础篇

Unit 1　Linguistics　/ 3
　　Text A　The Language Fossils Buried in Every Cell of Your Body　/ 3
　　Text B　Decoding Human Languages by Chimpanzees　/ 7

Unit 2　Astronomy　/ 12
　　Text A　This Database Gives Us the First Glimpse at What Diverse Worlds Out There Could Look Like　/ 12
　　Text B　Astronomers May Have Found Most Powerful Supernova　/ 17

Unit 3　Psychology　/ 21
　　Text A　Empathy: An Essential Element for a Successful Marriage　/ 21
　　Text B　Psychology of Eye Contact: Etiquette Rules You Should Know　/ 25

Unit 4　Culture　/ 29
　　Text A　Why Do the British Say "Sorry" So Much?　/ 29
　　Text B　Town Hopes Art Will Heal Trauma, and Raise Funds to Repair Flood Damage　/ 33

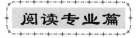

Unit 1　Mechanical Engineering　/ 39
　　Text A　Dutch Scientists Invent Bicycle That Warns You if You Are about to Crash　/ 39
　　Text B　Roboy: Switzerland's First Robotic Child!　/ 43

Unit 2　Automotive Engineering　/ 47
　　Text A　Five Facts on Electric Cars　/ 47

Text B　HOV Access Is Key for California Plug-in Car Purchases　／51
Unit 3　Civil Engineering　／55
　　　Text A　What Is Civil Engineering?　／55
　　　Text B　The Villa Savoye　／59
Unit 4　Electrical and Computer Engineering　／63
　　　Text A　China's Tianhe-2 Supercomputer Rated No.1 on the Top 500　／63
　　　Text B　NFC Tags　／67
Unit 5　Economics and Management　／71
　　　Text A　China's Money Outflow Not Investment Withdrawal: Authority　／71
　　　Text B　How Mounting Job Cuts Could Threaten the UK's Economic Recovery
　　　　　　　／75
Unit 6　Food and Chemical Engineering　／80
　　　Text A　Secret Air Pollutants in Our Homes Claim Thousands of Lives　／80
　　　Text B　Norwegian Confectioner Improves Safety and Efficiency　／84
Unit 7　Art and Design　／88
　　　Text A　Michelangelo　／88
　　　Text B　Chanel　／92

应用文写作

Unit 1　Manual　／99
Unit 2　Resume　／104
Unit 3　Notice　／113
Unit 4　Type of Letters　／118
Unit 5　Abstract　／124
Unit 6　Reference　／130

Appendix　／133
　　1. 常见院系名称双语对照　／133
　　2. 常见大学专业学科双语对照　／134
　　3. 常见专业技术职称名称双语对照　／136
　　4. 常见公司企业各部门名称双语对照　／138

参考答案及解析　／139
Glossary　／158

阅读基础篇

Unit 1

Linguistics

Text A

The Language Fossils Buried in Every Cell of Your Body

Voice can't be inherited like fossils; this makes studies of language origin be more difficult. But the charm of human languages still inspires explorers to **advance wave upon wave**.

A British family with a bizarre speech **deficit** has led linguists to FOXP2: a gene that begins to explain how our ancestors acquired languages.

It is a shame that grammar leaves no fossils behind. Few things have been more important to our evolutionary history than languages. Because our ancestors could talk to each other, they became a powerfully cooperative species. In modern society we are so **submerged** in words—spoken, written, signed, and texted—that they seem inseparable from human identity. And yet we cannot **excavate** some fossils from an Ethiopian hillside, point to a bone, and declare, "This is where languages began."

Lacking **hard evidence**, scholars of the past speculated broadly about the origin of languages. Some claimed that it started out as cries of pain, which gradually **crystallized** into distinct words. Others traced it back to music, to the **imitation** of animal grunts, or to birdsong. In 1866 the Linguistic Society of Paris got so **exasperated** by these **unmoored musings** that it banned all communication on the origin of languages. Its English counterpart felt the same way. In 1873 the president of the Philological Society of London declared that linguists "shall do more by tracing the historical growth of one single work-a-day tongue, than by filling wastepaper baskets with reams of paper covered with **speculations** on the origin of all tongues".

A century passed before linguists had a serious **change of heart**. The change came as they began to look at the deep structure of the language itself. MIT linguist Noam Chomsky asserted that the way children acquire languages is so effortless that it must have a biological foundation. Building on this idea, some of his colleagues argued that the language is an adaptation shaped by **natural selection**, just like eyes and wings. If so, it should be possible to find **clues** about how human languages evolved from grunts or **gesture**s by observing the communication of our close primate relatives. (353 words)

(http://article.yeeyan.org/view/202015/230433)

 Words and Expressions

1.	deficit	/ˈdefɪsɪt/	n.	缺陷;赤字;亏空
2.	submerge	/səbˈmɜːdʒ/	v.	淹没;沉浸
3.	excavate	/ˈekskəveɪt/	v.	挖掘;开凿
4.	crystallize	/ˈkrɪstəlaɪz/	v.	结晶;使(想法、信仰等)明确
5.	imitation	/ˌɪmɪˈteɪʃən/	n.	模仿;仿制品
6.	exasperate	/ɪɡˈzæspəreɪt/	v.	使恼怒;使恶化
7.	speculation	/ˌspekjuˈleɪʃən/	n.	推断;投机;思考
8.	clue	/kluː/	n.	线索;提示
9.	gesture	/ˈdʒestʃə(r)/	n.	手势;姿势
10.	advance wave upon wave			前赴后继
11.	hard evidence			真凭实据
12.	unmoored musings			天马行空
13.	change of heart			改变心意;改变看法
14.	natural selection			自然选择;物竞天择

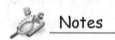 Notes

1. It is a shame that grammar leaves no fossils behind. Few things have been more important to our evolutionary history than languages. Because our ancestors could talk to each other, they became a powerfully cooperative species.

语法没有留下化石是件遗憾的事。对于我们人类的进化史来说,没什么东西比语言的出现更为重要,正是因为我们的祖先可以通过语言互相交流,人类之间的互助合作才显得更加强大有力。

2. In 1873 the president of the Philological Society of London declared that linguists "shall do more by tracing the historical growth of one single work-a-day tongue, than by filling wastepaper baskets with reams of paper covered with speculations on the origin of all tongues".

1873年,伦敦语言学协会的主席宣布语言学家们"应该致力于探寻某一日常语言的历史发展过程,而不应对所有语言的起源做那些吃力不讨好的无端揣测——这些揣测的文字最终都只能被扔进废纸篓里"。

3. MIT (Massachusetts Institute of Technology)

麻省理工学院,简称麻省理工,坐落于美国马萨诸塞州剑桥市(大波士顿地区),是世界著名的私立研究型大学,被誉为"世界理工大学之最"。麻省理工学院素以世界顶尖的工程学和计算机科学享誉世界,位列2015—2016年世界大学学术排名(ARWU)工程学世界第一、计算机科学世界第二。麻省理工学院与斯坦福大学、加州大学伯克利分校一同被称为工程科技界的学术领袖,在工程学和计算机科学方面,三所学校长期占据世界大学学术排名、US News最佳研究生院等权威排名的前3名。

4. MIT linguist Noam Chomsky asserted that the way children acquire languages is so effortless that it must have a biological foundation. Building on this idea, some of his colleagues argued that the language is an adaptation shaped by natural selection, just like eyes and wings. If so, it should be possible to find clues about how human languages evolved from grunts or gestures by observing the communication of our close primate relatives.

麻省理工的语言学家诺姆·乔姆斯基认为,儿童之所以可以轻松地习得语言,一定有其生物学基础。在这一观点的基础上,乔姆斯基的一些同事提出了他们的主张——语言的进化就像眼睛和翅膀一样,也是物竞天择的结果。果真如此的话,通过观察与我们亲缘关系最近的灵长类动物之间的沟通交流,就可能从中发现某些线索,证明人类语言到底是怎样从咕哝有声或者打手势进化而来的。

Exercises

I. Structure Analysis

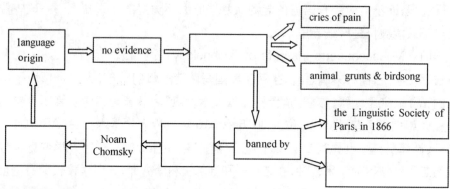

II. Term Matching

Directions: Match the English terms with their Chinese equivalents.

1. advance wave upon wave   a. 语言起源
2. speech deficit   b. 真凭实据
3. language origin   c. 痛苦哭喊
4. cries of pain   d. 前赴后继
5. hard evidence   e. 语言缺陷
6. change of heart   f. 生物基础
7. unmoored musings   g. 天马行空
8. trace back   h. 物竞天择
9. biological foundation   i. 改变看法
10. natural selection   j. 追溯

III. Reading Comprehension

Directions: Choose the best answer to each of the following questions.

(   ) 1. What makes the study of language origin be more difficult?
  A. The academic circle doesn't allow to study.
  B. The study of language origin is illegal.
  C. There are fewer explorers in this field.
  D. The voice can't be inherited like fossils.

(   ) 2. The speculations think that languages may originate from the imitation of _____.
  A. birdsong   B. music
  C. cries of pain   D. all of the above

( ) 3. Why did societies ban all studies of language origin?

    A. Because the studies spent too much.

    B. Because the studies led unmoored musings.

    C. Because the studies made people not work.

    D. Because the studies disordered the society order.

( ) 4. What did linguist Noam Chomsky assert?

    A. Human languages originated from 6 million years ago.

    B. Humans can study languages only when they are born.

    C. Humans study languages with a biological foundation.

    D. All of the above.

( ) 5. The language is an adaptation shaped by _____.

    A. historical evolution   B. natural selection

    C. weather condition   D. society development

Text B

Decoding Human Languages by Chimpanzees

Is the language unique to humans? Scientists are trying to find out the answer from chimpanzees, the animals which are the most similar to humans. Although previous studies have revealed that chimps could communicate with gestures, there has been no detailed study clearly showing what their each gesture means. Recently, a new study has decoded the expression of wild chimpanzees' body languages. It is the first time to write a "dictionary" for wild chimpanzees. The study also provides clues for the origin of human language study.

The study is accomplished by researchers from School of **Psychology and Neurosciencep** of the University of St Andrews, Scotland, and published in the international **authoritative** academic journal *Current Biology*.

The scientists discovered that wild chimps communicate 19 specific messages to one another with a "**lexicon**" of 66 gestures by following and filming communities of chimps in Uganda's Budongo Forest Reserve, and examining more than 5,000 incidents of these meaningful exchanges. "Only humans and chimps," Dr Catherine Hobaiter, who led the research, said, "had a system of communication where they deliberately sent a message to another individual."

Although previous research has revealed that apes and monkeys can understand complex information from another animal's call, the animals do not appear to use their voices intentionally to communicate messages. This was a **crucial** difference between calls and gestures, Dr Hobaiter said.

Some of the chimps' gestures, the researchers say, are **unambiguous**—used consistently to **convey** one meaning. Leaf **clipping**, for example, where a chimp very obviously takes small bites from leaves is used only to **elicit** sexual **attention**. Many others, though, appear to be ambiguous. A grab, for example, is used for: "Stop that", "Climb on me", and "Move away". Although many are very **subtle**, some of the footage captured by the researchers shows very clearly what the chimps mean to convey. "The big message is that there is another species out there that is meaningful in its communication, so that's not unique to humans," said Dr Hobaiter.

The study not only successfully researches in a large number of natural posture language of wild chimpanzees, but also provides valuable reference to trace the origin of human languages.

Dr Susanne Shultz, an **evolutionary biologist** from the University of Manchester, said the study was commendable in seeking to **fill the gaps** in our knowledge of the evolution of human languages. But, she added, the results were "a little disappointing". Because the **vagueness** of the gesture meanings suggest either that the chimps have little to communicate, or we are still missing a lot of the information contained in their gestures and actions. "Moreover, the meanings seem to not go beyond what other less **sophisticated** animals convey with **non-verbal** communication," she said. "So, it seems the gulf remains." (457 words)

(http://www.bbc.com/news/science-environment-28023630)

Unit 1　Linguistics

Words and Expressions

1.	chimpanzee	/ˌtʃɪmpænˈziː/	n.	黑猩猩
2.	authoritative	/ɔːˈθɒrətətɪv/	adj.	权威的；有权利的
3.	lexicon	/ˈleksɪkən/	n.	词典；专门词汇
4.	crucial	/ˈkruːʃl/	adj.	关键性的；决定性的
5.	unambiguous	/ˌʌnæmˈbɪɡjuəs/	adj.	不含糊的，清楚的
6.	convey	/kənˈveɪ/	v.	传达；运送；表达
7.	clipping	/ˈklɪpɪŋ/	n.	修剪；剪掉
8.	subtle	/ˈsʌtl/	adj.	微妙的；敏感的；巧妙的
9.	vagueness	/ˈveɪɡnɪs/	n.	含糊，不清楚
10.	sophisticated	/səˈfɪstɪkeɪtɪd/	adj.	复杂的；精致的；老于世故的
11.	non-verbal	/ˌnɑːnˈvɜːbl/	adj.	不使用语言的；非语言交际的
12.	psychology and neuroscience			心理学和神经科学
13.	elicit one's attention			吸引某人注意
14.	evolutionary biologist			进化生物学家
15.	fill the gap			填补空白；弥补缺陷

Notes

1. The scientists discovered that wild chimps communicate 19 specific messages to one another with a "lexicon" of 66 gestures by following and filming communities of chimps in Uganda's Budongo Forest Reserve, and examining more than 5,000 incidents of these meaningful exchanges.

科学家通过跟踪和拍摄乌干达布顿戈森林保护区的野生黑猩猩，记录下了超过5000例有意义的交流，发现野生黑猩猩使用了66种姿势语言，可以表达19种特定的意思。

2. Some of the chimps' gestures, the researchers say, are unambiguous—used consistently to convey one meaning. Leaf clipping, for example, where a chimp very obviously takes small bites from leaves is used only to elicit sexual attention. Many others, though, appear to be ambiguous.

研究人员说，黑猩猩的有些动作是清楚的——一直只表达一种意思。例如，黑猩猩把树叶撕咬成小片只是为了吸引异性注意。然而，还有很多动作的意思是含糊不清的。

3. The study not only successfully researches in a large number of natural posture language of wild chimpanzees, but also provides valuable reference to trace the origin of human languages.

这项研究的意义不仅仅在于对野外黑猩猩的大量自然姿势语言进行成功的研究,更在于这一研究结果能够为追溯人类语言的起源提供非常有价值的参考。

4. Dr Susanne Shultz, an evolutionary biologist from the University of Manchester, said the study was commendable in seeking to fill the gaps in our knowledge of the evolution of human languages. But, she added, the results were "a little disappointing". Because the vagueness of the gesture meanings suggest either that the chimps have little to communicate, or we are still missing a lot of the information contained in their gestures and actions.

一位曼彻斯特大学的进化生物学家苏珊娜·舒尔茨博士说,这项研究是值得称道的,它填补了我们在人类语言进化方面知识的空白。她也补充说,研究结果"有点令人失望"。因为含糊不清的手势含义表明也许是黑猩猩交流极少,也许是我们遗漏了很多包含在它们的手势和动作中的信息。

Exercises

I. Reading Comprehension

Directions: Judge whether each of the following statements is true(T) or false(F) according to the text, and correct the mistakes in the false statements.

(   ) 1. Previous studies have not only revealed chimps could communicate with posture, but also showed each posture meaning.

Modification:

(   ) 2. Scientists have spent a lot on studying chimpanzees' posture language because they are the most similar animals to humans.

Modification:

(   ) 3. Scientists have interpreted and categorized all chimpanzees' posture into 66 kinds of expression.

Modification:

(   ) 4. Biting leaves into strips is in order to capture other chimpanzees' attention to fight for territory.

Modification:

(   ) 5. Dr Susanne Shultz thought that the study was not perfect, because we still have a lot unaccountable.

Modification:

II. Questions for Discussion

Directions: Answer the following questions with the information contained in Text B.

1. What have previous studies revealed about animals' language?
2. What is the purpose of research on chimpanzees' gesture language?
3. What did scientists do to study chimpanzees' gesture language?
4. What's your opinion on the language origin?

Unit 2

Astronomy

Text A

This Database Gives Us the First Glimpse at What Diverse Worlds Out There Could Look Like

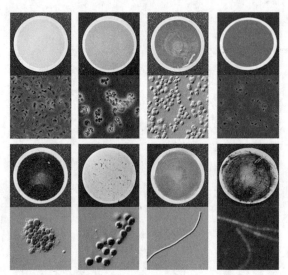

While looking for life on planets beyond our solar system, a group of international scientists has created a colorful **catalog** containing **reflection signatures** of Earth life-forms that might be found on planet surfaces throughout the cosmic hinterlands. The new database and research gives humans a better chance to learn if we are not alone.

"This database gives us the first glimpse at what diverse worlds out there could look like," said Lisa Kaltenegger from Cornell University. "We looked at a broad set of life forms, including some from the most extreme parts of Earth."

Along with Kaltenegger, the **interdisciplinary** team consists of Siddharth Hegde of the Max Planck Institute for Astronomy, and Ivan G. Paulino-Lima, Ryan Kent, and

Lynn Rothschild, all from NASA Ames Research Center.

"Much of the history of life on Earth has been dominated by **microbial** life," the scientists explained. "It is likely that life on **exoplanets** evolves through single-celled stages prior to multicellular creatures. Here, we present the first database for a diverse range of life, including **extremophiles** (organisms living in extreme conditions) found in the most inhospitable environments on Earth—for such surface features in preparation for the next generation of telescopes that will search for a wide variety of life on exoplanets."

To spot the tint of Earth, alien astronomers from a nearby star might measure light shimmering off the surface of a planet as sunlight reflected from our planet's vegetation reaches their telescopes. Conversely, astronomers here can see **pigmentation** on exoplanets and determine their makeup by looking at their color. "On Earth, these are just **niche** environments, but on other worlds, these life forms might just have the right makeup to dominate, and now we have a database to know how we could spot that," said Kaltenegger.

The group has gathered the cultures of 137 cellular life forms that range from Bacillus gathered at the Sonoran Desert to Halorubrum chaoviator found at Baja California, Mexico, to Oocystis minuta obtained in an oyster pond at Martha's Vineyard.

"Our results show the amazing diversity of life that one can detect remotely on exoplanets," said Hegde, an incoming Cornell research associate. "We explore for the first time the reflection signatures of a diversity of **pigmented microorganisms** isolated from various environments on Earth, including extreme ones, which will provide a broader guide, based on Earth life, for the search for surface features of **extraterrestrial** life." (398 words)

(http://www.astronomy.com/news/2015/03/colorful-life-form-catalog-will-help-discern-if-were-alone)

Words and Expressions

1.	database	/ˈdeɪtəbeɪs/	n.	数据库,资料库,信息库
2.	catalog	/ˈkætəlɔːg/	n.	目录;目录册,目录簿
3.	interdisciplinary	/ˌɪntəˈdɪsəplɪnəri/	adj.	跨学科的,多学科的
4.	microbial	/maɪˈkrəʊbɪəl/	adj.	微生物的,由细菌引起的
5.	exoplanet	/ekˈsɒplænɪt/	n.	外星球

6.	extremophile	/eksˈtreməˌfaɪl/	n.	极端微生物,极端生物;族群
7.	pigmentation	/ˌpɪgmenˈteɪʃən/	n.	天然颜色;色素沉着
8.	niche	/nɪtʃ/	n.	生态位(一个生物所占据的生境的最小单位)
9.	pigmented	/pɪgˈmentɪd/	adj.	天然色的;本色的
10.	microorganism	/ˌmaɪkrəʊˈɔːgənɪzəm/	n.	微生物
11.	extraterrestrial	/ˌekstrətəˈrestrɪəl/	adj.	地球外的;外星球的;宇宙的
12.	reflection signature			反射特征

 Notes

1. Here, we present the first database for a diverse range of life, including extremophiles (organisms living in extreme conditions) found in the most inhospitable environments on Earth—for such surface features in preparation for the next generation of telescopes that will search for a wide variety of life on exoplanets.

这里,我们首次提供了一个包含多种生物的数据库,这包括在地球上最荒凉的环境中发现的极端微生物(生活在极端环境下的生物体)。探索这样的地表特征有利于发展下一代可以探索外星球上多种生物的天文望远镜。

2. To spot the tint of Earth, alien astronomers from a nearby star might measure light shimmering off the surface of a planet as sunlight reflected from our planet's vegetation reaches their telescopes.

为了找出地球的印迹,附近星球的外星人天文学家们会在太阳光从地球植物反射至其望远镜时来探测在地球表面闪烁的光芒。

3. The group has gathered the cultures of 137 cellular life forms that range from Bacillus gathered at the Sonoran Desert to Halorubrum chaoviator found at Baja California, Mexico, to Oocystis minuta obtained in an oyster pond at Martha's Vineyard.

该研究小组已收集了137种生物机体的培养细胞,这包括在索诺兰沙漠发现的杆菌,在墨西哥的下加利福尼亚发现的盐红菌,以及在马萨葡萄园岛一个牡蛎塘里获得的卵胞藻。

4. We explore for the first time the reflection signatures of a diversity of pigmented microorganisms isolated from various environments on Earth, including extreme ones, which will provide a broader guide, based on Earth life, for the search for surface features of extraterrestrial life.

我们首次探测了各种隔绝于地球上不同生态环境的有色微生物的反射特征,这些微生物也包含了极端微生物。此次探测以地球生物为依据,为今后探索外星球的地貌特征提供了一个更广泛的指导。

Exercises

Ⅰ. Structure Analysis

About the Database

• What is the database?

The database is _____ containing _____ that might be found on planet surfaces throughout the cosmic hinterlands.

• Why is the database created?

(1) This database gives people the first glimpse at _____.

(2) It will provide a broader guide, based on Earth life, for the search for surface features of _____.

• Who creates the database?

(1) _____ from Cornell University;

(2) _____ of the Max Planck Institute for Astronomy;

(3) _____ from NASA Ames Research Center.

• What does the database include?

(1) It includes _____ of a diversity of _____ isolated from various environments on Earth, including extreme ones.

(2) It includes the cultures of 137 _____.

• How does the database work?

Astronomers on Earth can see pigmentation on exoplanets and determine _____ _____. The database offers a colorful catalog for astronomers to let them know how they could spot that makeup.

Ⅱ. Term Matching

Directions: Match the English terms with their Chinese equivalents.

1. database   a. 微生物

2. catalog   b. 天然颜色;色素沉着

3. extraterrestrial   c. 数据库,资料库,信息库

4. pigmented   d. 外星球

5. microbial   e. 跨学科的,多学科的

6. niche   f. 微生物的,由细菌引起的

7. exoplanet   g. 目录;目录册,目录簿

8. interdisciplinary   h. 地球外的;外星球的;宇宙的

9. pigmentation   i. 生态位

10. microorganism   j. 天然色的;本色的

Ⅲ. Reading Comprehension

Directions: Choose the best answer to each of the following questions.

( ) 1. Why did the scientists create this new database?

     A. To know what Earth life-forms could look like.

     B. To give humans a chance to learn that they are not alone.

     C. To find out different life-forms on our planet surface.

     D. To know what diverse worlds out there could look like.

( ) 2. What does the underlined word "inhospitable" mean in the fourth paragraph?

     A. Desert.   B. Unfriendly.   C. Unpleasant.   D. Hospital.

( ) 3. According to the fourth and the fifth paragraphs, which of the following statements is TRUE?

     A. Life on exoplanets evolves from single-celled stages to multicellular creatures.

     B. Much of the life on Earth has been dominated by microbic life.

     C. Astronomers on Earth cannot see pigmentation on exoplanets and determine their makeup.

     D. The next generation of telescopes fails to search for the life on exoplanets.

( ) 4. Where did the group of scientists find Oocystis minuta?

     A. In Baja California.   B. In Martha's Vineyard.

     C. In the Sonoran Desert.   D. In Mexico.

( ) 5. Which of the following statements is TRUE?

     A. The research shows that one cannot detect the life on exoplanets in a long distance.

     B. Hegde has been a research associate for a long time.

     C. The scientists have explored the reflection signatures of microorganisms in the extreme environments on Earth many times.

     D. The research can provide a broader guide for the search for surface features of the life on exoplanets.

Text B

Astronomers May Have Found Most Powerful Supernova

An international team of astronomers may have discovered the biggest and brightest supernova ever.

The **explosion** was 570 billion times brighter than the sun and 20 times brighter than all the stars in the **Milky Way galaxy** combined, according to a statement from the Ohio State University, which is leading the study. Scientists are straining to define its strength.

"This may be the most powerful supernova ever seen by anybody ... it's really **pushing the envelope** on what is possible," study co-author Krzysztof Stanek, an astronomer at Ohio State, was quoted as saying in *The Los Angeles Times*.

The team of astronomers released their findings this week in the journal *Science*. The explosion and a gas cloud that resulted are called ASASSN-15lh after the team of astronomers, All Sky Automated Survey for Supernovae, discovered it last June.

A supernova is a rare and often dramatic phenomenon that involves the explosion of most of the material within a star. Supernovas can be very bright for a short time and usually release huge amounts of energy.

Searching for the power source

This **blast** created a massive ball of hot gas that the astronomers are studying through telescopes around the world, Ohio State said. It cannot be seen with the naked eye because it is 3.8 billion light years from the Earth.

There's an object about 10 miles across in the middle of the ball of gas that astronomers are trying to define.

"The honest answer is at this point that we do not know what could be the power source for ASASSN-15lh," said Subo Dong, lead author of the *Science* paper, according to Ohio State. He is a Youth Qianren Research Professor of Astronomy at the Kavli Institute for Astronomy and Astrophysics at Peking University.

Todd Thompson, professor of astronomy at Ohio State, said the object in the center may be a rare type of star called a **millisecond magnetar**. **Spawned** by a supernova, it's a rapidly spinning, dense star with a powerful magnetic field.

Could it be a "**supermassive** black hole"?

To achieve the brightness recorded, the magnetar would have to spin 1,000 times a second and "convert all that **rotational** energy to light with nearly 100% efficiency," Thompson said, according to the Ohio State press release. "It would be the most extreme example of a magnetar that scientists believe to be physically possible."

The question of whether a suprnova truly caused the space explosion may be settled later this year with help from the Hubble Space Telescope, which will allow astronomers to see the host galaxy surrounding the object in center of the ball of gas, Ohio State said.

If it's not a magnetar, it may be unusual nuclear activity around "a supermassive black hole", Ohio State said. (458 words)

(http://edition.cnn.com/2016/01/14/us/possible-powerful-supernova/index.html)

Words and Expressions

1.	supernova	/ˌsuːpəˈnəʊvə/	n.	（天文）超新星
2.	explosion	/ɪkˈspləʊʒn/	n.	爆发；爆炸，炸裂
3.	galaxy	/ˈɡæləksi/	n.	星系；银河系
4.	blast	/blɑːst/	n.	爆炸
5.	millisecond	/ˈmɪlisekənd/	n.	毫秒
6.	magnetar	/ˈmæɡnɪtɑː/	n.	（有很强磁场的）中子星
7.	spawn	/spɔːn/	v.	引起
8.	supermassive	/ˈsjuːpəmæsɪv/	adj.	特大质量的
9.	rotational	/rəʊˈteɪʃənl/	adj.	转动的
10.	Milky Way			银河
11.	push the envelope			挑战极限

Notes

1. The explosion was 570 billion times brighter than the sun and 20 times brighter than all the stars in the Milky Way galaxy combined, according to a statement from the Ohio State University, which is leading the study.

该研究的牵头者俄亥俄州立大学称,此次爆炸所发出的光亮是太阳的5700亿倍,是银河系中所有星体总光度的20倍。

2. "This may be the most powerful supernova ever seen by anybody ... it's really pushing the envelope on what is possible," study co-author Krzysztof Stanek, an astronomer at Ohio State, was quoted as saying in *The Los Angeles Times*.

引用该报告的其中一位作者,来自俄亥俄州立大学的天文学家克日什托夫·施塔内克在《洛杉矶时报》中说的话:"这也许是人类有史以来看到的最具威力的超新星……这表明它将有可能推翻我们之前所知的一切。"

3. To achieve the brightness recorded, the magnetar would have to spin 1,000 times a second and "convert all that rotational energy to light with nearly 100% efficiency," Thompson said, according to the Ohio State press release.

据俄亥俄州立大学发布的新闻称,要达到该记录的亮度,中子星每秒须旋转1000次。汤姆森还称:"(中子星)须将旋转的能量几乎百分百地转化为光亮才行。"

4. The question of whether a suprnova truly caused the space explosion may be settled later this year with help from the Hubble Space Telescope, which will allow astronomers to see the host galaxy surrounding the object in center of the ball of gas, Ohio State said.

俄亥俄州立大学称,他们将在今年晚些时候,利用哈勃太空望远镜来解答是不是超新星引起太空爆炸的。哈勃太空望远镜可以让天文学家看到该球状气体中心物质的寄主星系。

Exercises

I. **Reading Comprehension**

Directions: Judge whether each of the following statements is true(T) or false(F) according to the text, and correct the mistakes in the false statements.

( ) 1. The explosion was 20 times brighter than most of the stars in the Milky Way galaxy combined.

Modification:

( ) 2. All Sky Automated Survey for Supernovae discovered ASASSN-15lh this week.

Modification:

(   ) 3. A supernova does not occur very often.

Modification:

(   ) 4. The ball of gas created by the explosion cannot be seen with the naked eye because it is too far away from the Earth.

Modification:

(   ) 5. The astronomers have defined the object in the middle of the ball of gas.

Modification:

Ⅱ. **Questions for Discussion**

Directions: Answer the following questions with the information contained in Text B.

1. What are the characteristics of a supernova?
2. Have the scientists found out the power source of the blast?
3. What is the function of the Hubble Space Telescope?
4. What's your opinion on the discovery of this supernova?

Unit 3
Psychology

Text A

Empathy: An Essential Element for a Successful Marriage

It is our ability to take in another's experience and feel it in our own brain and body. It is the practice of understanding another person's condition from their perspective. Empathy is a necessary component of any positive relationship, and particularly a marriage.

The term empathy was first introduced in 1909 by psychologist Edward B. Titchener as a translation of the German term *einfühlung* (meaning "feeling into"). Different from **sympathy**, empathy generally involves a much more active attempt to understand another person and leads to helping behavior, which benefits social relationships. Empathy is not only a kind of personality trait, but also a kind of psychological process.

Resonance, also emotional empathy, means feeling in one's own body that someone else is experiencing. It can be explained by the existence of "**mirror neurons**". Mirror neurons are in the parts of our brain that react to emotions expressed by others and then reproduce those same emotions within ourselves. These neurons could help explain how and why we "read" other people's minds and understand what they are feeling.

The next process, **cognitive empathy**, concerns putting oneself in someone else's shoes. It is the ability to take someone else's perspective and understand the effect their viewpoint has on their emotions.

Self-regulation is an important skill that regulates your emotions so as not to experience your own personal distress at the **disclosure** of someone else's distress. For example, when you hear about someone's grief or anguish, you do not take it on yourself and become distressed. This understanding of someone's feelings does not involve you having your own bad reaction to those feelings.

Build **healthy boundaries.** Marriage needs a **semi-permeable** boundary that allows friends and family to contact with you but that doesn't interfere with your own desires and plans. It is essential to the concept of "differentiation".

Differentiation is an ability to separate thought from feeling. The more **well-differentiated** people are, the more **resilient** they will be and the healthier and more sustaining their relationships will be.

These four **neurological** processes work **synergistically** within you to create genuine empathy, which help partners to have an understanding of each other's **family of origin** experience, and evoke empathy around unmet needs and reasons why current situations trigger strong reactions. (375 words)

(http://marriage.about.com/od/marriagetoolbox/fl/Empathy-An-Essential-Element-For-a-Successful-Marriage.htm)

Words and Expressions

1.	empathy	/ˈempəθi/	n.	同感；共鸣；同情
2.	sympathy	/ˈsɪmpəθi/	n.	同情
3.	resonance	/ˈrezənəns/	n.	共鸣
4.	self-regulation	/ˌselfˌreɡjʊˈleɪʃən/	n.	自我调控
5.	disclosure	/dɪsˈkləʊʒə(r)/	n.	揭露
6.	semi-permeable	/ˌsemiˈpɜːmiəbl/	adj.	半渗透的
7.	well-differentiated		adj.	分化良好的
8.	resilient	/rɪˈzɪliənt/	adj.	恢复快的
9.	neurological	/ˌnjʊərəˈlɒdʒɪkl/	adj.	神经的
10.	synergistically	/ˌsɪnəˈdʒɪstɪkəli/	adv.	协同作用地
11.	mirror neuron			镜像神经元
12.	cognitive empathy			认知移情
13.	healthy boundary			健康界线
14.	family of origin			原生家庭

1. Different from sympathy, empathy generally involves a much more active attempt to understand another person and leads to helping behavior, which benefits social relationships. Empathy is not only a kind of personality trait, but also a kind of psychological process.

与同情不同的是,共鸣通常指更积极主动地尝试理解他人,并产生助人行为,这有助于社会关系的发展。共鸣既是一种人格特质,也是一种心理过程。

2. Mirror neurons are in the parts of our brain that react to emotions expressed by others and then reproduce those same emotions within ourselves.

镜像神经元作为人类大脑的组成部分,对他人表达的情感给予反应并在自身产生相同的情感。

3. Self-regulation is an important skill that regulates your emotions so as not to experience your own personal distress at the disclosure of someone else's distress. For example, when you hear about someone's grief or anguish, you do not take it on yourself and become distressed. This understanding of someone's feelings does not involve you having your own bad reaction to those feelings.

自我调控是一项重要的技能,它使你在了解别人的不幸遭遇时,能及时调整自我情绪以免陷入自身的痛苦经历中。例如,在你听到使他人难过的事情时,你不会让自己也陷入难过的情绪中。理解他人情感的同时不会使自身陷入由那些情感带来的不良反应中。

4. differentiation

"分化"一词,最先是用来形容细胞的分化,不同的细胞有不同的功能,却又紧密地依附在同一组织里面。后来心理学家弗洛伊德将自我分化纳入精神分析理论术语中,指个体出生后,在与环境接触的过程中,逐渐从最原始的本我中分化出自我,在行为上也逐渐由本能冲动变为接受现实规范的约束,能够将理智与情感区分开,这是个体在原生家庭中开始形成并逐渐稳定的一种行为反应倾向,能够在广泛的情境中对个体的行为进行预测,并影响个体的心理健康。

5. Differentiation is an ability to separate thought from feeling. The more well-differentiated people are, the more resilient they will be and the healthier and more sustaining their relationships will be.

分化是指个体能够将理智与情感区分开的能力,人们的分化能力越好,精神状态恢复就越快,他们的婚姻关系就越健康持久。

Exercises

Ⅰ. Structure Analysis

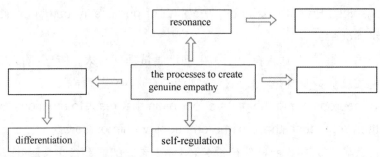

Ⅱ. Term Matching

Directions: Match the English terms with their Chinese equivalents.

1. family of origin   a. 镜像神经元
2. differentiation   b. 同感；共鸣
3. self-regulation   c. 自我调控
4. mirror neuron   d. 共鸣
5. resonance   e. 原生家庭
6. healthy boundary   f. 分化
7. empathy   g. 健康界线

Ⅲ. Reading Comprehension

Directions: Choose the best answer to each of the following questions.

(   ) 1. What is the difference between sympathy and empathy?

    A. Sympathy involves a much active understanding of other people.

    B. Empathy is a necessary component of any relationship.

    C. Empathy involves a passive attempt.

    D. Empathy can lead to an active helping behavior, which is good for social relationship.

(   ) 2. What can help us explain how and why we understand what others are feeling?

    A. Mirror neurons.　　　　　　B. Resonance.

    C. Empathy.　　　　　　　　　D. Sympathy.

(   ) 3. If someone is not good at self-regulation, what will happen?

    A. He will put himself in others' shoes.

    B. He will fall into his distress experience while hearing others' distress.

C. He will be very happy all the time.

D. He will be resilient during a conversation.

( ) 4. How do you understand "differientiation" in psychology?

A. Differientiation is nonsignificant for healthy relationship.

B. Differientiation involves the division of cells.

C. A well-differiented person can not deal with the relationship with others.

D. A well-differiented person has an ability to separate thoughts from feelings.

Text B

Psychology of Eye Contact: Etiquette Rules You Should Know

Eye contact, as a socialising device, is the most immediate and noticeable nonverbal message you can send to others. The **self-assurance** and confidence conveyed by direct eye contact put both parties at ease within a conversation.

Generally in Western societies, eye contact is expected to be regular but not overly **persistent**. Constant eye contact is often considered to be **intimidation**, causing the person to feel overly studied and uncomfortable. Even between humans and non-humans, persistent eye contact is sometimes **unadvisable**: the *New Zealand Medical Journal* reported that one reason why so many young children fall to attacks by pet dogs is their over-poweringly constant eye contact with pets, which causes them to feel threatened and be defensive.

But when you fail to look at a person in the eye, it usually means you are hiding something. Even if it is only because you are shy or nervous, it will seem dishonest and deceitful.

To maintain a healthy level of eye contact, a few etiquette rules about it should be kept in mind. This positioning may be the most appropriate in a business situation. Imagine a line below your business associates' eyes. This will serve as the base of a triangle and the peak will be at their mid-forehead. Keep your eyes in the middle of that triangle when speaking to others. On a personal level, **invert** the triangle so that its peak is now at their mouth. Still, keep your eyes focused in the middle of the triangle, which is now at the bridge of their nose.

Also, spending too much time looking at the triangle may give off inappropriate nonverbal messages. Communication experts recommend the appropriate amount of eye contact should be a series of long glances instead of intense stares, looking someone in the eye for **intervals** of four to five seconds, then looking away briefly—in the middle of the triangle—then re-establish eye contact.

Then, control the blink rate in eye contact. Aside from the **instinctive** need to blink, the emotions and feelings towards the person people are talking to can **subconsciously** cause the alteration of blink rate. If you're trying to send a serious message, you should practice your direct eye contact without blinking, because limited blinking adds to your message's credibility. Blinking more than the average 6–10 times per minute can be a good indicator that a person is attracted to the person they're talking to, and is for this reason used as a sign of **flirting**.

Understanding the psychology of eye contact can help you successfully cultivate relationships, personal and professional. You can demonstrate an interest in others by interacting in the conversation and maintaining eye contact at healthy intervals. (455 words)

(https://www.psychologistworld.com/bodylanguage/eyes.phphttp://www.businessinsider.com/8-etiquette-rules-you-need-to-know-about-eye-contact-2013-10)

Words and Expressions

1.	self-assurance	/ˌselfəˈʃʊərəns/	n.	自信
2.	persistent	/pəˈsɪstənt/	adj.	持续的
3.	intimidation	/ɪnˌtɪmɪˈdeɪʃən/	n.	恐吓
4.	unadvisable	/ˌʌnədˈvaɪzəbl/	adj.	不妥当的
5.	invert	/ɪnˈvɜːt/	vt.	使反转
6.	interval	/ˈɪntəvl/	n.	间隔
7.	instinctive	/ɪnˈstɪŋktɪv/	adj.	本能的
8.	subconsciously	/ˌsʌbˈkɒnʃəsli/	adv.	潜意识地
9.	flirt	/flɜːt/	vi.	调情

Notes

1. Even between humans and non-humans, persistent eye contact is sometimes unadvisable: the *New Zealand Medical Journal* reported one reason why so many young children fall to attacks by pet dogs is their over-poweringly constant eye contact with pets, which causes them to feel threatened and be defensive.

甚至在人类和非人类之间,有时候持续的眼神接触都是不妥当的。《新西兰医学期刊》曾报道如此多的小孩被宠物狗袭击的一个原因就是他们和宠物之间长时间压制性的眼神接触使宠物感到受到威胁而进行自卫。

2. Imagine a line below your business associates' eyes. This will serve as the base of a triangle and the peak will be at their mid-forehead. keep your eyes in the middle of that triangle when speaking to others.

想象在你商务伙伴的眼睛下方有一条线,这条线作为三角形的底边,前额中间为顶点。当交流时眼神聚焦在三角形的中央。

3. Communication experts recommend the appropriate amount of eye contact should be a series of long glances instead of intense stares, looking someone in the eye for intervals of four to five seconds, then looking away briefly—in the middle of the triangle—then re-establish eye contact.

交际学专家建议眼神接触要保持适度,应该是一系列的略视,而不是强烈的凝视。眼神接触以四到五秒钟为一个间隔,简短地转移视线,然后回到三角区中央,再重建眼神接触。

4. Aside from the instinctive need to blink, the emotions and feelings towards the person people are talking to can subconsciously cause the alteration of blink rate.

除了本能需要眨眼睛外,对正在交谈的人产生的情绪和情感也会改变眨眼频率。

Exercises

Ⅰ. Reading Comprehension

Directions: Judge whether each of the following statements is true(T) or false(F) according to the text, and correct the mistakes in the false statements.

(   ) 1. Persistent eye contact is expected in Western societies.
Modification:

(   ) 2. The dog will not hurt you even if you intimidate it with constant eye contact.

Modification:

(   ) 3. When you avoid eye contact in a conversation, you are regarded as dishonest or deceitful even if you are shy or nervous.

Modification:

(   ) 4. When you send a serious message, limited blinking can add to your message's credibility.

Modification:

(   ) 5. You can always keep your eyes in the middle of triangle when talking to others.

Modification:

II. Questions for Discussion

Directions: Answer the following questions with the information contained in Text B.

1. Why is eye contact very important?
2. How to control the amount of eye contact according to the communication experts?
3. Does blinking have another meaning besides the instinctive need?

Unit 4

Culture

Text A

Why Do the British Say "Sorry" So Much?

A recent survey of over 1,000 British found that the average person says "sorry" around eight times per day—and that one in eight people apologise up to 20 times a day. What's the reason for this **peculiar** verbal **tic**?

"There's **speculation** that Canadians and British apologise more than Americans, but it's difficult to study in a way that would provide any **compelling** evidence," says a psychologist.

The origins of the word "sorry" means "distressed, grieved or full of sorrow", but most British people use the word more casually and often. But this doesn't necessarily mean they're more **remorseful**.

"We can use it to express empathy—so I might say 'sorry about the rain'," says Battistella. "It might be that British and Canadian speakers use that kind of 'sorry' more often, but they wouldn't be apologising, **per se**."

British society values that its members show respect without **imposing** on someone else's personal space, and without drawing attention to oneself: which refers to as "negative-politeness". America, on the other hand, is a positive-politeness society, characterised by friendliness and a desire to feel part of a group.

Consequently, the British may sometimes use "sorry" in a way that can seem inappropriate to outsiders. They will say "sorry" to someone they don't know because they'd like to ask for some information, or to sit down next to them—and because not saying "sorry" would constitute an even greater **invasion** of that stranger's **privacy**.

"Our excessive, often inappropriate and sometimes **downright** misleading use of this word **devalues** it, and it makes things very confusing and difficult for foreigners **unaccustomed** to our ways," says Fox. Still. She adds, "I don't think saying 'sorry' all the time is such a bad thing. It even makes sense in the context of a negative-politeness culture."

There may be other benefits to saying "sorry", too—such as **fostering** trust. In one study, Brooks recruited a male actor to approach 65 strangers at a train station on a rainy day and ask to borrow their telephones. In half of the cases, the actor preceded his request with: "Sorry about the rain." When he did this, 47% of strangers gave him their mobiles, compared to only 9% when he simply asked to borrow their phones. "By saying 'I'm sorry about the rain', the **superfluous** apologiser acknowledges an unfortunate circumstance, takes the victim's perspective and expresses empathy for the negative circumstance," says Wood Brooks. (400 words)

(http://www.bbc.com/future/story/20160223-why-do-the-british-say-sorry-so-much)

Words and Expressions

1.	peculiar	[pɪˈkjuːliə(r)]	adj.	特有的
2.	tic	/tɪk/	n.	不随意的、突然发生的、快速的、反复出现的、无明显目的的、非节律性的运动或发声
3.	speculation	/ˌspekjuˈleɪʃən/	n.	推断
4.	compelling	/kəmˈpelɪŋ/	adj.	非常强烈的；不可抗拒的
5.	remorseful	/rɪˈmɔːsfl/	adj.	懊悔的
6.	per se	/ˌpɜːˈseɪ/	adv.	本质上
7.	impose	/ɪmˈpəʊz/	vi.	施加影响，迫使
8.	invasion	/ɪnˈveɪʒn/	n.	侵犯
9.	privacy	/ˈprɪvəsi/	n.	隐私

10.	downright	/ˈdaʊnraɪt/	adv.	完全地,彻底地
11.	devalue	/ˌdiːˈvæljuː/	vt.	贬低
12.	unaccustomed	/ˌʌnəˈkʌstəmd/	adj.	不习惯的
13	foster	/ˈfɒstə(r)/	vt.	培养;促进
14	superfluous	/suːˈpɜːfluəs/	adj.	过多的

Notes

1. "There's speculation that Canadians and British apologise more than Americans, but it's difficult to study in a way that would provide any compelling evidence," says a psychologist.

"据推断,与美国人相比,加拿大人和英国人道歉的次数更多,但是要找到获取这个强有力的证据的方法是很难的,"一位心理学家说。

2. negative-politeness

逆向的礼貌手段是与正面的礼貌手段相对而言的,是从相反的方向来满足人们维护自己尊严的诉求。当我们的言谈涉及批评、建议、要求或命令时,意味着我们的言谈可能会伤及他人的面子和自尊,此时我们就要用逆向的、间接的礼貌手段,尽量保全他人的颜面,尽量避免或减少可能引起的冲突,以达到更好的交流效果。文中的negative-politeness是指以不打扰别人的个人空间这种不过问的、间接的做法来达到对他人礼貌的目的。

3. positive-politeness

用赞美等手段正面满足人们展示自己美好一面的诉求。

4. British society values that its members show respect without imposing on someone else's personal space, and without drawing attention to oneself, which refers to as "negative-politeness".

英国社会注重以不打扰个人空间、不过分关注来表示对他人的尊重,这叫作"间接礼貌手段"。

Exercises

I. Structure Analysis

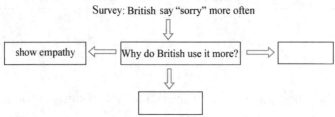

II. Term Matching

Directions: Match the English terms with their Chinese equivalents.

1. unaccustomed to   a. 陌生人的隐私
2. speculation   b. 过多道歉的人
3. compelling evidence   c. 逆向的礼貌手段
4. foster trust   d. 推断
5. negative politeness   e. 注意到
6. superfluous apologiser   f. 侵犯
7. draw attention to   g. 不习惯
8. stranger's privacy   h. 培养信任感
9. invasion   i. 强有力的证据
10. peculiar verbal tic   j. 特有的口头禅

III. Reading Comprehension

Directions: Choose the best answer to each of the following questions.

(　　) 1. What's NOT the reason for British saying "sorry"?
    A. To show empathy.　　　　B. To show regret.
    C. To show sorrow.　　　　 D. To show off.

(　　) 2. Canadians and British use "sorry" most for _____.
    A. being distressed　　　　B. being remorseful
    C. sharing empathy　　　　 D. apologizing

(　　) 3. Which of the following situations do you think indicate the British's negative-politeness in public?
    A. Care about "group".
    B. Pay no attention to what others are doing.
    C. Neglect others' difficulties.

D. Care about only "me".

( ) 4. What do you think most Americans will NOT do according to the passage?

A. Join the new neighbour's house-warming party.

B. Hold a welcome party for newcomers.

C. Retire quietly without letting co-workers know.

D. Join the Chinese New Year parade.

( ) 5. Which of the following is TRUE?

A. British feel regretful more often than Americans.

B. British use "sorry" to replace "excuse me" in some occasions.

C. "Sorry" helps to make a good impression of you in social activities.

D. British believe that people will think they are well-educated when they say sorry more often.

Text B

Town Hopes Art Will Heal Trauma, and Raise Funds to Repair Flood Damage

Residents of a flood-struck community have turned to art to heal the trauma of the event, and boost spirits in the community. In Darwin, a huge **mural** tells the stories of floods that struck a remote community on Boxing Day.

The work is a community effort with Nauiyu artists collaborating to create the painting. "My aunty did this painting of the helicopter picking up men and women," Kieren said, pointing at the mural. "I painted this snake and crocodile because they were swimming around the community."

The town's art centre opened a **pop-up stall** in Darwin, selling fabrics, homewares and clothes aiming to boost commissions to help repair damages to the centre.

"My house was **inundated**. The water was knee-deep. Clothes and bed got damaged. We had to throw everything out. It was all dirty, muddy and smelly after the floods," a resident said.

The floodwaters swept through the town in December 2015, and on Boxing Day almost 500 Nauiyu residents were **evacuated** to Darwin's Foskey Pavilion showgrounds for more than two weeks.

It was the third-longest running evacuation in Australian history. The NT Government acknowledged things could have been done differently and was conducting a review. "We needed to put extra toilets in. We would like to put temporary facilities in so people can do their own washing. It wasn't till about the third day we activated the night **patrol** to assist the security of the pavilion," said Collene Bremner, the Department of Chief Minister Director of Emergency Recovery. She also remarked that the community had given some ideas for communication improvements in the future, such as introducing a siren when flood waters are rising quickly.

Flood **mitigation** works were also under consideration, however ultimately, the location of the town meant it was **susceptible** to more flooding in the future. Much of the community has been cleaned up and Ms. Bremner said the clean-up was quicker and more efficient than the 2011 floods due to a more **coordinated** effort.

After the **devastating** Boxing Day flood at the community, residents have turned to art as a way to tell the story and rebuild their lives.

Artist McTaggart said there was a lot of disappointment in the community about the way the flood evacuations were conducted. Consultation and communication was lacking and some residents in the community felt their voices were not heard. Bremner hoped next time the process could be more community-driven. "We will look at going-into-the-community and developing-a-community action plan for a flood event," she told the ABC.

However Mr. McTaggart was **sceptical**: "I don't know if the plan will work." Artists hoped the pop-up arts store would raise enough money to repair damage caused by the floods and boost **morale**. (459 words)

(http://www.abc.net.au/news/2016-02-19/town-turns-to-art-to-tell-story-of-boxing-day-flood/7185688? site =indigenous&topic =latest)

Words and Expressions

1.	trauma	/ˈtrɔːmə/	n.	创伤
2.	mural	/ˈmjʊərəl/	n.	(大型)壁画
3.	pop-up	/ˈpɒpˌʌp/	adj.	弹起的
4.	stall	/stɔːl/	n.	货摊
5.	inundate	/ˈɪnʌndeɪt/	vt.	淹没
6.	evacuate	/ɪˈvækjueɪt/	vt.	疏散,撤离
7.	patrol	/pəˈtrəʊl/	n.	巡逻
8.	mitigation	/ˌmɪtɪˈɡeɪʃən/	n.	缓解,减轻

9.	susceptible	/sə'septəbl/	adj.	易受影响的
10.	coordinated	/kəu'ɔːdɪneɪtɪd/	adj.	协调的
11.	devastating	/'devəsteɪtɪŋ/	adj.	灾难性的
12.	sceptical	/'skeptɪkl/	adj.	怀疑的
13.	morale	/mə'rɑːl/	n.	士气

 Notes

1. Boxing Day

节礼日,为每年的12月26日,圣诞节次日或是圣诞节后的第一个星期日,大英国协旗下国家,包括英国、爱尔兰、澳大利亚、新西兰及加拿大,都把这天定为节日并举行纪念庆典。在这一日传统上要向服务业工人赠送圣诞节礼物,这些礼物通常被称为"圣诞节盒子"(Christmas Boxes),所以英文的"节礼日"译为"Boxing Day"。而今,很多商家冬季打折活动是从这一天开始的,所以这一天现在也被认为是购物节。

2. "… It wasn't till about the third day we activated the night patrol to assist the security of the pavilion," said Collene Bremner, the Department of Chief Minister Director of Emergency Recovery.

"……直到第三天我们才启动夜巡来确保馆内的安全,"紧急重建部门下属的首席部长主任克兰尼·布兰那说。

3. Flood mitigation works were also under consideration, however ultimately, the location of the town meant it was susceptible to more flooding in the future.

防洪减灾工作也在被考虑中,但基本上,小镇的地理位置决定了它将会受到更多的洪水影响。

4. Consultation and communication was lacking and some residents in the community felt their voices were not heard.

缺少咨询和沟通工作,社区内一些成员感觉自己的诉求并没有得到满足。

Exercises

I. Reading Comprehension

Directions: Judge whether each of the following statements is true(T) or false(F) according to the text, and correct the mistakes in the false statements.

(   ) 1. Kieren has painted turtle, helicopter, snake and crocodile on the mural.

Modification:

(　　) 2. The stall in Darwin sells fabrics, housewares, clothes and paintings.
Modification:

(　　) 3. During the evacuation, the government had set up the alarming system.
Modification:

(　　) 4. Flood mitigation works were in construction.
Modification:

(　　) 5. According to Bremner's state, the flood evacuation work needed improvements.
Modification:

II. Questions for Discussion

Directions: Answer the following questions with the information contained in Text B.

1. Do you think the community will recover from the flood by the artists' effort? Why or why not?

2. What measurements would you take to help the community after the flood if you were the officials?

3. What can the community do to minimise the loss resulting from frequent floods?

4. What can the artists do to "boost morale" for the residents, besides selling their products?

阅读专业篇

Unit 1
Mechanical Engineering

Text A

Dutch Scientists Invent Bicycle That Warns You if You Are about to Crash

The Netherlands on Monday launched its first-ever "**intelligent bicycle**", fitted with an array of electronic devices to help bring down the high accident rate among elderly cyclists in the bicycle-mad country.

Developed for the government by **the Netherlands Organization for Applied Scientific Research (TNO)**, the intelligent bicycle **prototype** runs on electricity, and sports a forward-looking **radar** mounted below the handlebars and a camera in the **rear mudguard**.

A commercial-available bicycle is expected to be on the market in the next two years and should sell for between 1,700 euros to 3,200 euros per bicycle.

The forward and rearward detection devices on the test bike are linked through an on-board computer with a **vibrating warning system** installed in the bicycle's **saddle** and handlebars to alert cyclists to **impending** danger.

The saddle vibrates when other cyclists approach from behind, while the handlebars do the same when obstacles appear ahead.

It also has a **cradle** in which a **computer tablet** can be inserted, to wirelessly connect and "talk" to the bicycle through a dedicated application.

The mounted tablet also flashes a bright signal if there is an approaching obstacle in the bicycle's path, like a lamppost, or if another cyclist comes up from behind intending to pass.

"Accidents often happen when cyclists look behind them or get a fright when they are passed at high speed," said Maurice Kwakkernaat, one of TNO's research scientists involved in the project.

"The **on-board system** utilities technology already at work in the automotive industry," he said.

Kwakkernaat said the devices would be useful for cyclists **propelled** along by the bicycle's electrical motor, which can reach a top speed of 25 kph (about 16 mph).

"More and more elderly people are using a bicycle, not only for short distances, but also for longer distances," Dutch Environment and Infrastructure Minister Melanie Schultz van Haegen told AFP.

"This type of bicycle is truly needed in the Netherlands because it will help us down bring the number of elderly people who are injured every year and allow them to continue enjoying cycling," she said. (356 words)

(http://language.chinadaily.com.cn/news/2014-12/17/content_19108494.htm)

Words and Expressions

1.	prototype	/ˈprəʊtətaɪp/	n.	原型
2.	radar	/ˈreɪdɑː(r)/	n.	雷达
3.	rear	/rɪə(r)/	adj.	后方的
4.	mudguard	/ˈmʌdɡɑːd/	n.	(自行车)挡泥板
5.	saddle	/ˈsædl/	n.	车座
6.	impending	/ɪmˈpendɪŋ/	adj.	即将发生的
7.	cradle	/ˈkreɪdl/	n.	吊架,支架,吊篮
8	on-board	/ˈɒnˈbɔːd/	adj.	随车携带的
9.	propel	/prəˈpel/	vt.	推进
10.	intelligent bicycle			智能自行车

11.	the Netherlands Organization for Applied Scientific Research (TNO)	荷兰应用科学研究院
12.	vibrating warning system	振动警报系统
13.	computer tablet	平板电脑
14.	on-board system	车载系统

Notes

1. Developed for the government by the Netherlands Organization for Applied Scientific Research (TNO), the intelligent bicycle prototype runs on electricity, and sports a forward-looking radar mounted below the handlebars and a camera in the rear mudguard.

"智能自行车"是由荷兰政府委托荷兰应用科学研究院开发的。这款原型机依靠电力运行,车把下方装有前视雷达,后方挡泥板上装有一台相机。

2. The forward and rearward detection devices on the test bike are linked through an on-board computer with a vibrating warning system installed in the bicycle's saddle and handlebars to alert cyclists to impending danger.

测试车的前置和后置检测装备通过机载计算机与振动警报系统相连接。内置在自行车车座和车把中的振动警报系统,能够提醒骑自行车者可能发生的危险。

3. The mounted tablet also flashes a bright signal if there is an approaching obstacle in the bicycle's path, like a lamppost, or if another cyclist comes up from behind intending to pass.

当道路上有障碍物,如灯柱,或者当另外一个骑自行车者从后方出现并打算超过时,这个平板电脑也会发出明亮的闪烁信号。

4. "More and more elderly people are using a bicycle, not only for short distances, but also for longer distances," Dutch Environment and Infrastructure Minister Melanie Schultz van Haegen told AFP.

荷兰环境与基础建设部部长梅拉妮·舒尔茨·凡·哈根对法新社记者表示:"越来越多的老年人开始骑自行车,短途和长途的都有。"

Exercises

Ⅰ. **Structure Analysis**

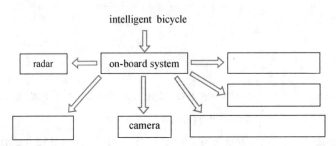

Ⅱ. **Term Matching**

Directions: Match the English terms with their Chinese equivalents.

1. intelligent bicycle   a. 荷兰应用科学研究院
2. computer tablet   b. 机载系统
3. TNO   c. 平板电脑
4. rearward detection device   d. 智能自行车
5. on-board system   e. 后置检测装备
6. rear mudguard   f. 吊架,支架,吊篮
7. vibrating warning system   g. 车座
8. handlebar   h. 振动警报系统
9. cradle   i. 后挡泥板
10. saddle   j. 车把

Ⅲ. **Reading Comprehension**

Directions: Choose the best answer to each of the following questions.

(   ) 1. Why did the Netherlands launch the "intelligent bicycle"?
   A. To help reduce the rate of accidents.
   B. To do more intelligent things.
   C. To match the need of elderly cyclists.
   D. To protect the environment.

(   ) 2. What does the intelligent bicycle prototype run on?
   A. Petrol.   B. Manpower.
   C. Electric power. D. Hybrid.

(   ) 3. What is the function of the vibrating warning system?
   A. It is the power of the bicycle.

B. To avoid the danger happening in the road.

C. It is the massage on the body.

D. To protect cyclists.

( ) 4. What can the cradle do in the intelligent bicycle?

A. It can install a computer tablet.

B. It can "talk" to the bicycle.

C. It can also hold something you need.

D. All of the above.

( ) 5. According to Maurice Kwakkernaat, when do accidents often happen?

A. When people pass through the road.

B. When cyclists ride at high speed.

C. When cyclists feel frightened.

D. When cyclists look behind them or get a fright when they are passed at high speed.

Text B

Roboy: Switzerland's First Robotic Child!

In celebration of the 25th anniversary of the Artificial Intelligence Laboratory (AI Lab) Zurich, the University of Zurich presents "Robots on Tour": World Congress & Exhibition of Robots, **Humanoids**, **Cyborgs** and more. It took place on the 8th (only for schools) and the 9th (public exhibition with approx 4,000 visitors) in Zurich, Switzerland. Over 40 robots from all over the world such as AFFETTO, iCub, Armar, PR-2 and Cornell Ranger will be presented to the broad audience. World-class speakers attended and as an additional highlight, the AI Lab **unveiled** its new robot.

If robots are going to be part of our everyday lives, they'll need to **fit into** our homes rather than the factory floor. Few people would be comfortable living with a metal spider on **tank treads**, so the University of Zurich's AI Lab has built this robot **toddler** called "Roboy".

Using "**soft robotics**" technology that **mimics** the human body, the 1.2 meter-tall humanoid robot is part of an effort to make robots that people are more comfortable with in day-to-day situations.

Roboy doesn't look very **endearing** at the moment. In fact, it looks more like a cyborg skeleton than a charming child, but it's still a work in progress. The laboratory's goal is to build Roboy in only nine months. Work began with 15 project partners and over 40 engineers and scientists. These parties are providing expertise and funds through sponsorship and **crowd funding** that includes **auctioning** space on the robot for logos, and hiring it out for business functions when completed.

Built out of plastic, Roboy is **modeled on** the human **musculoskeletal** system, but this mimicry goes beyond the aesthetic. Instead of motors in its joints, Roboy uses motor assemblies that pull **elastic cables**, so the system operates in a way similar to muscles and **tendons**. The AI Lab claims that this will allow Roboy to move "almost as elegantly as a human".

The purpose of Roboy is to push for the acceptance of service robots by making people more comfortable having them around all the time. With an aging population, the AI Lab believes that such service robots will be increasingly important in helping the elderly to continue independent lives.

Roboy is currently getting a new face chosen by a Facebook contest, and can move its arms. Later, the robot will be covered with a soft skin. Roboy has made its first public appearance at the "Robots on Tour" exhibition to celebrate the AI Lab's 25th anniversary, and next it aims to make more people accept and like it. (429 words)

(http://language.chinadaily.com.cn/2013-06/20/content_16560980.htm)

Words and Expressions

1.	humanoid	/ˈhjuːmənɔɪd/	n.	仿真机器人；类人动物
2.	cyborg	/ˈsaɪbɔːg/	n.	半人半机器的生物
3.	unveil	/ˌʌnˈveɪl/	vt.	使公之于众
4.	toddler	/ˈtɒdlə(r)/	n.	学步的幼儿
5.	mimic	/ˈmɪmɪk/	vt.	模仿
6.	endearing	/ɪnˈdɪərɪŋ/	adj.	令人爱慕的；惹人喜爱的
7.	auction	/ˈɔːkʃən/	v.	竞卖，拍卖
8.	musculoskeletal	/ˌmʌskjʊləʊˈskelətəl/	adj.	肌(与)骨骼的
9.	tendon	/ˈtendən/	n.	筋，腱

Unit 1　Mechanical Engineering

10.	fit into	适合,适应
11.	tank tread	坦克履带
12.	soft robotic	软机器人技术(指机器人在形态、功能上对人体的模拟)
13.	crowd funding	群众集资
14.	model on	仿照……制作
15.	elastic cable	弹性电缆

  Notes

1. Roboy

机器小子：是一款人形科研机器人的名称,是单词"robot"(机器人)和"boy"(男孩)的合成词。它可以完成如转弯、前进、侧步、前滚翻、后滚翻、鞠躬、俯卧撑、仰卧起坐等基本的仿人动作,还可以完成如街舞表演、体操表演等一组动作。机器人配置姿态平衡传感器,摔倒后可自主站立起来。

2. It took place on the 8th (only for schools) and the 9th (public exhibition with approx 4,000 visitors) in Zurich, Switzerland. Over 40 robots from all over the world such as AFFETTO, iCub, Armar, PR-2 and Cornell Ranger will be presented to the broad audience.

这次大型展会在瑞士的苏黎世举办,并作为第八届学生专场和第九届公众场吸引了大约4000名参观者。来自全世界的四十多个机器人,如 AFFETTO、iCub、Armar、PR-2 和 Cornell Ranger 将在展会上与广大观众见面。

3. Few people would be comfortable living with a metal spider on tank treads, so the University of Zurich's AI Lab has built this robot toddler called "Roboy".

很少有人能接受家里有个靠履带行走的金属蜘蛛,因此苏黎世大学人工智能实验室把家用机器人设计成孩子的形象,并亲切地叫它"机器小子"。

4. Built out of plastic, Roboy is modeled on the human musculoskeletal system, but this mimicry goes beyond the aesthetic.

"机器小子"是基于人体肌肉骨骼系统用塑料进行建模的,但它的这种模拟远远超出了人们的审美。

5. The purpose of Roboy is to push for the acceptance of service robots by making people more comfortable having them around all the time.

"机器小子"的问世会推进服务机器人的普及。让人们感觉到,服务机器人可以一直给他们的生活带来更多的便捷。

Exercises

I. Reading Comprehension

Directions: Judge whether each of the following statements is true(T) or false(F) according to the text, and correct the mistakes in the false statements.

(   ) 1. Robots will pay more attention to fitting into the industrial production in the future.
Modification:

(   ) 2. There is no need for improvement since Roboy has become available firstly.
Modification:

(   ) 3. Roboy can be used for commercial purposes by sponsors.
Modification:

(   ) 4. The motors of Roboy will be installed in the joints.
Modification:

(   ) 5. It is the "soft robotics" technology that Roboy uses to imitate the human body.
Modification:

II. Questions for Discussion

Directions: Answer the following questions with the information contained in Text B.

1. What do you think is the purpose of Roboy?
2. How does Roboy work almost as elegantly as a human?
3. In what way do researchers raise money for this project?
4. What's your opinion on the creation of Roboy?

Unit 2
Automotive Engineering

Text A

Five Facts on Electric Cars

How much do you know about electric cars? Check out these five quick facts:

Batteries can go dead just like **gas tanks** can go empty. This fact has resulted in much range anxiety among **prospective** electric car buyers and in fact, has also contributed to the popularity of **hybrid cars**. But just like other batteries, car batteries can be recharged. It is generally recommended that electric cars be **plugged in** overnight for a full **charge**, but charging stations are beginning to be put into place that would allow an electric car to become charged in as few as 20 minutes, though there is concern the "quick charge" doesn't last as long as an overnight charge.

Owning an electric car doesn't mean you must own a second car unless you frequently need to travel long distances. Hybrid electric cars, because they can go unlimited distances by relying on an on-board gas **combustion engine**, can be an **alternative** if that's the case. Range of electric cars can vary and is affected by things like weight and driving habits.

Electric cars tend to be smaller than **conventional** cars. However, they are equally as safe as gas-powered cars of the same class. The reason why many cars are small is due to the low energy **density** of batteries and the tie in between weight and range.

Electric cars can be pricier than their conventional **counterparts**. While the price of an **EV** is set by market forces, and some have argued that electric cars should be priced lower than conventional because on an **equivalent** production basis, they are cheaper to build with fewer parts. Electric cars can also be cheaper to maintain for the same reason, though they do require the purchase of a replacement battery about every 4 to 5 years.

Electric cars have multiple benefits. They provide a quieter ride with less air pollution.

They are also less costly to operate, something to keep in mind if your favorite electric car falls slightly out of your budget range. Electric cars should be more reliable since they have fewer parts. And while the idea of an electric car may seem new, in reality, they have been around for nearly 150 years. (371 words)

(http://alternativefuels.about.com/od/electricvehicle1/a/Five-Facts-On-Electric-Cars.htm?utm_term=electric%20cars%202016&utm_content=p2-main-2-title&utm_medium=sem&utm_source=msn&utm_campaign=adid-63508e87-9c7f-4bd6-96a5-027637478666-0-ab_msb_ocode-31677&ad=semD&an=msn_s&am=broad&q=electric%20cars%202016&dqi=&o=31677&l=sem&gsrc=99&askid=63508e87-9c7f-4bd6-96a5-027637478666-0-ab_msb)

Words and Expressions

1.	battery	/ˈbætri/	n.	电池,蓄电池
2.	prospective	/prəˈspektɪv/	adj.	未来的;预期的
3	charge	/tʃɑːdʒ/	n.	电荷
4	alternative	/ɔːlˈtɜːnətɪv/	n.	二中选一;供替代的选择
5	conventional	/kənˈvenʃənl/	adj.	传统的;平常的
6	density	/ˈdensəti/	n.	密度
7	counterpart	/ˈkaʊntəpɑːt/	n.	配对物;极相似的人或物
8	equivalent	/ɪˈkwɪvələnt/	adj.	等价的,相等的
9	gas tank			汽车油箱
10	hybrid car			混合动力车;双动力车
11	plug in			插入(电源)

12	combustion engine	内燃机
13	EV	电动汽车

 Notes

1. This fact has resulted in much range anxiety among prospective electric car buyers and in fact, has also contributed to the popularity of hybrid cars.

这种情况已对预期电动汽车购买者造成了很大程度的焦虑,事实上,这也影响着混合动力车的受欢迎度。

2. It is generally recommended that electric cars be plugged in overnight for a full charge, but charging stations are beginning to be put into place that would allow an electric car to become charged in as few as 20 minutes, though there is concern the "quick charge" doesn't last as long as an overnight charge.

通常推荐整夜为电动汽车充电即为满电,尽管有人担忧"快充"没有整夜充那么耐用,但充电站即将开始投放使用,在这里,电动汽车充电只需要20分钟。

3. Hybrid electric cars, because they can go unlimited distances by relying on an on-board gas combustion engine, can be an alternative if that's the case.

如果那样的话,混合动力车可以是一种选择,因为它们可以依靠随车携带的汽油内燃机行驶任意的距离。

4. While the price of an EV is set by market forces, and some have argued that electric cars should be priced lower than conventional because on an equivalent production basis, they are cheaper to build with fewer parts.

虽然电动汽车的价格是由市场力量决定的,但是有些人提出电动汽车应该比传统汽车定价更低,因为基于等价的生产基础,它们只用更少的零件便能更便宜地被制造出来。

Exercises

Ⅰ. **Structure Analysis**

Five facts on electric cars:

1. Batteries can go dead just like gas tanks can go empty.

2. _____

3. _____

4. _____

5. Electric cars have multiple benefits. For example, a quieter ride with _____ _____.

Ⅱ. Term Matching

Directions: Match the English terms with their Chinese equivalents.

1. hybrid car   a. 再充电
2. EV   b. 等价的
3. gas tank   c. 混合动力车
4. combustion engine   d. 密度
5. counterpart   e. 配对物
6. alternative   f. 电动汽车
7. recharge   g. 油箱
8. on-board   h. 内燃机
9. equivalent   i. 替代物
10. density   j. 随车携带的

Ⅲ. Reading Comprehension

Directions: Choose the best answer to each of the following questions.

(   ) 1. According to the passage, what made the future electric car buyers anxious?
　　　A. Gas tanks can go empty.　　B. Batteries can go dead.
　　　C. Gas can be exhausted.　　　D. Batteries can be recharged.

(   ) 2. How long is it recommended that we fully charge an electric car?
　　　A. Less than 20 minutes.　　　B. 20 minutes.
　　　C. More than 20 minutes.　　　D. A full night.

(   ) 3. What kind of circumstances do you need a second car besides an electric car?
　　　A. You travel a lot by air.　　　B. You travel a lot by multiple vehicles.
　　　C. You frequently travel long distances.　D. You frequently travel short distances.

(   ) 4. What lets electric cars tend to be smaller than conventional cars?
　　　A. Low energy density of batteries.　　B. Weight.
　　　C. Range.　　　　　　　　　　　　　D. All of the above.

(   ) 5. Why should electric cars be cheaper than conventional cars?
　　　A. Because electric cars have fewer parts.
　　　B. Because conventional cars have fewer parts.
　　　C. Because they aren't on an equivalent production basis.
　　　D. Because electric is cheaper than gas.

Text B

HOV Access Is Key for California Plug-in Car Purchases

A UC Davis study published in April showed that a good third to almost 60 percent of California **plug-in vehicle** (**PEV**) purchases are primarily motivated by solo access to **high occupancy vehicle** (**HOV**) **lanes**—which can become **congested** at times.

California is the leader in PEV acceptance, and policy-makers adopting a **carrot-and-stick** approach of **incentives** and **perks** have long included stickers that give alternative-energy car buyers access to (usually) less congested lanes.

Last decade yellow stickers were adopted for hybrid vehicle applicants, and more recently, there have been green stickers for **transitional zero emission vehicles** (**TZEVs**) and white for Federal **Inherently Low Emission Vehicles** (**ILEVs**).

Researchers at the UC Davis Institute of Transportation Studies interviewed more than 3,500 California PEV owners in coordination with the California Center for **Sustainable** Energy administering the survey on behalf of the California Air Resources Board.

Out of 3,500 PEV owners or **lessors**, 3,000 said they applied for and received a green or white **decal**, and 500 did not.

The percentage of those who applied includes 95 percent Prius plug-in hybrid, 89 percent Chevy Volts, and 79 percent Nissan Leafs.

"When asked about their primary motivation to buy the car," wrote authors Gil Tal and Michael Nicholas, "57% of Plug-in Priuses, 34% of Volts and 38% of Leafs identified it as the HOV decal (a more recent 4Q 2013 analysis shows somewhat lower percentages—34%, 20%, and 15% respectively)."

Among other key findings, the authors discovered HOV access as the main purchase motivation is higher in the more densely congested Bay Area and Los Angeles than in other regions. These areas generally have more congestion on freeway and more HOV lanes available.

The study also confirmed more than 80 percent of PEVs are being used for **commuting**, and **BEVs** have a lower commute frequency than **PHEV** drivers.

Also, the study shows a higher frequency of Prius plug-in owners which reduces the number of electric miles in the HOV lane.

The study further found higher-income earners were more likely to take advantage of the HOV sticker perk. It is believed one reason is time is money to them, so saving minutes on busy freeways is a motivator.

In all, "the impact of the HOV decals as well as the state **rebate** is different for each household based on the location, travel needs, income and other socio economic variables," said the authors.

It's being **postulated** that the effectiveness of this benefit could be increased by prioritizing PHEVs with larger **all-electric** range and not to just any PHEV, particularly those with a short range such as the Prius rated at around 11 miles more or less. (448 words)

(http://www.hybridcars.com/hov-access-is-key-for-california-plug-in-car-purchases/)

Words and Expressions

1.	lane	/leɪn/	n.	车道;航线
2.	congested	/kənˈdʒestɪd/	adj.	拥挤的;堵塞的
3.	carrot-and-stick	/ˌkærətənˈstɪk/	adj.	威逼加利诱的;软硬兼施的
4.	incentive	/ɪnˈsentɪv/	n.	动机;刺激
5.	perk	/pɜːk/	n.	额外补贴
6.	sustainable	/səˈsteɪnəbl/	adj.	可持续的
7.	lessor	/leˈsɔː(r)/	n.	出租人
8.	decal	/ˈdiːkæl/	n.	贴花纸
9.	commute	/kəˈmjuːt/	vi.	乘公交车上下班
10.	rebate	/ˈriːbeɪt/	n.	折扣

11.	postulate	/ˈpɒstjuleɪt/	vt.	假定
12.	all-electric	/ˈɔːlɪˈektrɪk/	adj.	全电气化的
13.	plug-in vehicle (PEV)			电动汽车
14.	high occupancy vehicle (HOV)			高乘载汽车
15.	transitional zero emission vehicles (TZEVs)			过渡性零排放车辆
16.	Inherently Low Emission Vehicles (ILEVs)			固有低排放车辆
17.	BEVs (battery electric vehicles)			纯电动汽车
18.	PHEV (plug-in hybridelectric vehicle)			插电式混合动力汽车

 Notes

1. UC Davis (University of California, Davis)

加利福尼亚大学戴维斯分校,是位于萨克拉门托(Sacramento)西部的公立研究型大学,为全美最顶尖的公立大学之一,与加州大学伯克利分校(UC Berkeley)、加州大学洛杉矶分校(UCLA)、加州大学圣地亚哥分校(UC San Diego)并称"上流加州大学"(Upper UCs)。

2. A UC Davis study published in April showed that a good third to almost 60 percent of California plug-in vehicle (PEV) purchases are primarily motivated by solo access to high occupancy vehicle (HOV) lanes—which can become congested at times.

一份4月出版的加州大学戴维斯分校的研究表明有1/3到大约60%的加州电动汽车购买主要是源于单人驾车可使用偶尔堵塞的高乘载车辆车道。(HOV车道是美国、加拿大等国家为了提高道路使用率、缓解交通拥堵和促进交通节能减排而采用的交通管理措施。在这种车道上只能行驶公共汽车或"拼车"族的车或供乘坐两人以上的车辆使用,坐多名乘客的车辆可以免费通过收费桥梁或道路等。)

3. California is the leader in PEV acceptance, and policy-makers adopting a carrot-and-stick approach of incentives and perks have long included stickers that give alternative-energy car buyers access to (usually) less congested lanes.

在电动汽车接纳方面加州是领先者,政府决策者采取软硬兼施的激励和额外补贴的办法,其中长时间包括对选择动力车辆购买者发放能够驶入(通常)较少拥堵的车道的标签。

4. the California Air Resources Board

加州空气资源委员会

5. In all, "the impact of the HOV decals as well as the state rebate is different for

each household based on the location, travel needs, income and other socio economic variables," said the authors.

总之,作者们提道:"和国家退税一样,高乘载车辆标签的影响根据地点、旅行需求、收入和其他社会经济变量而对每个家庭都不同。"

Exercises

I. Reading Comprehension

Directions: Judge whether each of the following statements is true(T) or false(F) according to the text, and correct the mistakes in the false statements.

(　　) 1. It is indicated that about 30%–60% California PEV purchases are mainly motivated by solo access to HOV lanes.

Modification:

(　　) 2. As a leader of accepting PEV, California only uses rewards to promote PEV.

Modification:

(　　) 3. In Bay Area and Los Angeles, HOV access as the main purchase motivation is higher than in other regions.

Modification:

(　　) 4. PHEVs have a higher commute frequency than BEVs.

Modification:

(　　) 5. There is an assumption that the effectiveness of this benefit could be increased by all PHEVs.

Modification:

II. Questions for Discussion

Directions: Answer the following questions with the information contained in Text B.

1. What is the main reason why people in California tend to buy plug-in cars?
2. What kind of methods do the policy-makers adopt to promote PEVs in California?
3. Why is the HOV sticker perk useful for the higher-income earners?
4. If you want to buy a car, which one do you like, BEV or PHEV? Why?

Unit 3

Civil Engineering

Text A

What Is Civil Engineering?

Civil engineering is **arguably** the oldest engineering **discipline**. It deals with the built environment and can be dated to the first time someone placed a roof over his or her head or laid a tree trunk across a river to make it easier to get across. Civil engineering relates to human life greatly. It is the fact that civil engineers have saved more lives than all the doctors in history—development of clean water and **sanitation systems.**

The built environment **encompasses** much of what defines modern civilization. Buildings and bridges are often the first constructions that come to mind, as they are the most conspicuous creations of structural engineering, one of civil engineering's major sub-disciplines. Roads, railroads, subway systems, and airports are designed by transportation engineers, another category of civil engineering. And then there are the less visible creations of civil engineers. Every time you open a water **faucet**, you expect water to come out, without thinking that civil engineers made it possible. New York City has one of the world's most impressive water supply systems, receiving billions of gallons of high-quality water from the Catskills over one hundred miles away. Similarly, not many people seem to worry about what happens to the water after it has served its purposes. The old civil engineering discipline of sanitary engineering has evolved into modern environmental engineering of such significance that most **academic** departments have changed their names to civil and environmental engineering.

These few examples illustrate that civil engineers do a lot more than design buildings and bridges. They can be found in the **aerospace** industry, designing **jetliners** and space stations; in the automotive industry, perfecting the load-carrying capacity of a **chassis** and improving the **crashworthiness** of **bumpers** and doors; and they can be found in the ship-building industry, the power industry, and many other industries wherever constructed facilities are involved. And they plan and oversee the construction of these facilities as construction managers.

Civil engineering is an exciting profession because at the end of the day you can see the results of your work, whether this is a completed bridge, a high-rise building, a subway station, or a **hydroelectric dam**. (359 words)

(http://civil.columbia.edu/what-civil-engineering)

Words and Expressions

1.	arguably	/ˈɑːɡjuəbli/	adv.	可论证地
2.	discipline	/ˈdɪsəplɪn/	n.	学科
3.	encompass	/ɪnˈkʌmpəs/	vt.	包含，包括
4.	faucet	/ˈfɔːsɪt/	n.	水龙头
5.	academic	/ˌækəˈdemɪk/	adj.	学科的，学术的
6.	aerospace	/ˈeərəʊspeɪs/	n.	航空与航天
7.	jetliner	/ˈdʒetlaɪnə(r)/	n.	喷气客机
8.	chassis	/ˈʃæsi/	n.	(车辆的)底盘
9.	crashworthiness	/ˈkræʃˌwɜːðɪnəs/	n.	防撞性
10.	bumper	/ˈbʌmpə(r)/	n.	保险杠
11	sanitation system			卫生系统
12.	hydroelectric dam			水电站坝

Notes

1. It deals with the built environment and can be dated to the first time someone placed a roof over his or her head or laid a tree trunk across a river to make it easier to get across.

土木工程学研究建筑环境，最早可以追溯到人类第一次在头顶上盖起了屋顶或者是为了更容易跨过河流，在水面上放根树干的时候。

2. Buildings and bridges are often the first constructions that come to mind, as they are the most conspicuous creations of structural engineering, one of civil

engineering's major sub-disciplines.

楼房和桥梁是人们首先能想到的建筑，因为它们是最显而易见的建筑工程的成果，而建筑工程是土木工程学的一个主要分支学科。

3. The old civil engineering discipline of sanitary engineering has evolved into modern environmental engineering of such significance that most academic departments have changed their names to civil and environmental engineering.

原先土木工程学中的卫生工程学已经发展成为现代的环境工程学，这是非常重要的一门学科，很多大学的学院已经更名为土木与环境工程学院。

4. They can be found in the aerospace industry, designing jetliners and space stations; in the automotive industry, perfecting the load-carrying capacity of a chassis and improving the crashworthiness of bumpers and doors; and they can be found in the ship-building industry, the power industry, and many other industries wherever constructed facilities are involved.

航空航天业有土木工程师的身影，他们设计喷气客机和空间站；汽车工业有土木工程师的身影，他们让汽车底盘的承载能力更加完美并且改善保险杠和车门的防撞性能；在造船业、电力业以及其他许多涉及建筑设施的行业都有他们的身影。

Exercises

I. Structure Analysis

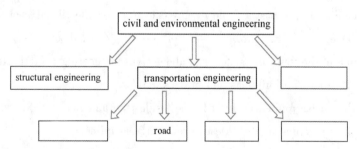

II. Term Matching

Directions: Match the English terms with their Chinese equivalents.

1. civil engineering   a. 建筑环境
2. sanitation system   b. 学科
3. built environment   c. (汽车)底盘
4. construction   d. 卫生系统
5. water supply system   e. 建筑物
6. discipline   f. 喷气客机

7. aerospace industry   g. 防撞性

8. jetliner   h. 土木工程学

9. chassis   i. 航空航天工业

10. crashworthiness   j. 供水系统

Ⅲ. Reading Comprehension

Directions: Choose the best answer to each of the following questions.

(　　) 1. What does civil engineering deal with?

    A. It deals with roofs and tree trunks.

    B. It deals with clean water and sanitation systems.

    C. It deals with buildings and bridges.

    D. It deals with the built environment.

(　　) 2. Why have civil engineers saved more lives than all doctors in history?

    A. Because they have developed clean water and sanitation systems.

    B. Because they have created roofs.

    C. Because they have created buildings and bridges.

    D. Because they have created buildings and roads.

(　　) 3. Which of the following are the less visible creations of civil engineers?

    A. Buildings and bridges.

    B. Roads, railways and subway systems.

    C. Water supply systems.

    D. Jetliners and space stations.

(　　) 4. According to the passage, how many categories does civil engineering fall into?

    A. One.   B. Two.   C. Three.   D. Four.

(　　) 5. Which of the following statements about civil engineering is NOT true?

    A. It deals with buildings and bridges only.

    B. It can be applied to many fields besides the automotive industry.

    C. It is regarded as the oldest engineering discipline.

    D. It encompasses structural engineering, transportation engineering and sanitary engineering.

The Villa Savoye

Introduction

Poissy is just under an hour's drive from Paris, and is typical of the suburbs of the capital, with long streets of single-family garden homes. The Villa Savoye **occupies** one of these sites, standing closer to nature than to the street and releasing a large green space around it (although the construction of facilities for the city after the war has weakened significantly in the area of private housing). The main part of the house (living-room, kitchen, bedrooms and bathrooms) is located on the first floor, while the ground floor is occupied by the hall and offices for the service. There is also a garage capable of storing 3 automobiles of the time on the ground floor, which was a **milestone** in the history of architecture and a great step forward for its time. The roof is flat and on it there is a small garden.

The ground floor is largely determined by the movement of a car entering the building. This movement also determines the structure, based on an **orthogonal grid** of **concrete** pillars separated 4.75 meters from each other. This forms a square grid of 23.5 meters on the side, on top of which sits the Villa.

The house was **inhabited** by its owners for a short period of time. The building was completed in 1929, but after the German invasion of France in 1940, it was abandoned and then bombed and burned during the Second World War. In 1963, the Villa Savoye was declared as "**architectural heritage**" by the French government, which then proceeded to restore it because it was in a state of neglect and ruin after the attacks in the war.

It is currently a "museum", dedicated to the life and works of **Le Corbusier** and maintained by the public company Monuments of France, and receives thousands of visits per year, mostly **architects** and students.

Concept

The Villa Savoye was designed by Le Corbusier as a **paradigm** of the "machine as a home", so that the functions of everyday life inside become critical to its design. The movement of cars to enter the interior of the house (a concept that **impassioned** Le Corbusier for years) is the **trigger** for the design of the building.

This concept also includes the fact that housing is designed as an object that **allegedly** landed on the landscape, is totally **autonomous** and it can be placed anywhere in the world. Architecture followed the style of airplanes, cars and ships, with the declared aim of achieving mass production of housing.

Pillars supporting the ground floor also advanced this idea, and the independence of the Villa from its garden, and was recognized as one of the key points of the first generation of international architecture. (452 words)

(https://en.wikiarquitectura.com/index.php/Villa_Savoye)

Words and Expressions

1	Poissy		n.	(法国）普瓦西
2	occupy	/ˈɒkjupaɪ/	vt.	占用
3	milestone	/ˈmaɪlstəʊn/	n.	里程碑
4	orthogonal	/ɔːˈθɒɡənl/	adj.	直角的
5	grid	/ɡrɪd/	n.	格子，格栅
6	concrete	/ˈkɒŋkriːt/	n.	混凝土
7	inhabit	/ɪnˈhæbɪt/	vt.	居住于
8	architect	/ˈɑːkɪtekt/	n.	建筑师
9	paradigm	/ˈpærədaɪm/	n.	范例，样式
10	impassion	/ɪmˈpæʃən/	vt.	激起热情
11	trigger	/ˈtrɪɡə(r)/	n.	起因，诱因
12	allegedly	/əˈledʒɪdli/	adv.	据说
13	autonomous	/ɔːˈtɒnəməs/	adj.	有自主权的

Unit 3　Civil Engineering

14	pillar	/ˈpɪlə(r)/	n.	柱,台柱
15	Villa Savoye		n.	萨伏伊别墅
16	architectural heritage			建筑遗产
17	Le Corbusier			勒科尔比西埃(1887—1965,旅居法国的瑞士建筑设计师)

Notes

1. Poissy is just under an hour's drive from Paris, and is typical of the suburbs of the capital, with long streets of single-family garden homes.

普瓦西离巴黎不到一个小时的车程,是典型的巴黎郊区,长长的街道上矗立着带着花园的独门独栋的房屋。

2. There is also a garage capable of storing 3 automobiles of the time on the ground floor, which was a milestone in the history of architecture and a great step forward for its time.

一楼还有一个车库,能够停放3辆当时的汽车,这在建筑历史上是个里程碑,在当时可谓是一个大进步。

3. This movement also determines the structure, based on an orthogonal grid of concrete pillars separated 4.75 meters from each other.

为了方便汽车的进出,别墅的底层结构设计为互成直角的钢筋混凝土柱子,每根柱子的间隔是4.75米。

4. It is currently a "museum", dedicated to the life and works of Le Corbusier and maintained by the public company Monuments of France, and receives thousands of visits per year, mostly architects and students.

萨伏伊别墅如今是展示勒科尔比西埃的生活与作品的博物馆,由一家叫作法国纪念碑的公共事业公司来维护,每年接待成千上万名游客,游客多数是建筑师和学生。

5. The Villa Savoye was designed by Le Corbusier as a paradigm of the "machine as a home", so that the functions of everyday life inside become critical to its design.

萨伏伊别墅堪称是勒科尔比西埃"机器如家"设计理念的典范,因此家居日常生活的功能是别墅设计的着眼点。

6. Architecture followed the style of airplanes, cars and ships, with the declared aim of achieving mass production of housing.

建筑与飞机、汽车和轮船的设计风格一样,其目的是实现楼房的大规模生产。

Exercises

I. Reading Comprehension

Directions: Judge whether each of the following statements is true(T) or false(F) according to the text, and correct the mistakes in the false statements.

(   ) 1. The main part of the Villa Savoye (living-room, kitchen, bedrooms and bathrooms) is located on the ground floor.

Modification:

(   ) 2. The design of the Villa Savoye was a milestone in the history of architecture and a great step forward for its time.

Modification:

(   ) 3. Le Corbusier's concept of the "machine as a home" means that we can make a machine as a house.

Modification:

(   ) 4. The Villa Savoye was originally a private house, but now it has become a "museum", which receives lots of visitors each year.

Modification:

(   ) 5. According to Le Corbusier, architecture should be constructed in a large scale as machines.

Modification:

II. Questions for Discussion

Directions: Answer the following questions with the information contained in Text B.

1. Where is the Villa Savoye located?
2. Why was the Villa Savoye recognized as the milestone in the history of architecture?
3. How do you understand Le Corbusier's concept of the "machine as a home"?
4. Can you collect more information about the Villa Savoy?

Unit 4
Electrical and Computer Engineering

Text A

China's Tianhe-2 Supercomputer Rated No.1 on the Top 500

China's Tianhe-2 supercomputer has just been rated No. 1 on the top 500—a respected list of the world's most powerful computers. Experts measured the supercomputer's performance at 33.86 **petaflop** or **quadrillion** of operations per second.

China's National University of Defense Technology developed the supercomputer, which runs twice as fast as the No. 2 rated Titan supercomputer. It belongs to the United States Government's Oak Ridge National Laboratory in Tennessee. Both Tianhe-2 and Titan are part of an **ongoing** race to make supercomputers faster and more powerful.

So what is a supercomputer? A basic personal computer has one **microchip** at the center of its operations. This Central Processing Unit, or CPU, **executes** a set of commands contained in a **predesigned** program. The first supercomputers had a few more CPUs. That number grew as **microprocessors** became  cheaper and faster. Andrew Grimshaw, a computer science professor at the University of Virginia explains: "Today, supercomputers are all what we call **parallel machines**. Instead of one CPU-central processing unit—they have thousands and thousands. And in the case of the Chinese machine, depending on how you count, millions of the central processing units." These parallel machines are made up of many individual computers called **nodes**. They are all positioned in one block. They use a lot of power, create a lot of heat, and require huge **cooling systems**. They also use programs different from those used by ordinary computers.

Professor Grimshaw says anyone with enough resources can build a supercomputer to solve problems that require millions of **mathematical calculations**.

But that's not always necessary. A **virtual** supercomputer can be created by networking individual computers within a university campus or company. These machines then process data during **down time**, when no one is using them.

"Those are very easy to run on virtual supercomputers because each problem is independent of all the others and I can **scatter** these jobs out all around the place. We run these all the time at UVA."

"It's transforming science and engineering, and it's going to continue to transform it in ways I think most people don't fully grasp—how well we can model and **simulate** the world now."

Professor Grimshaw says the increasing computing ability of supercomputers makes the future of research very bright. (382 words)

(http://www.putclub.com/html/radio/VOASPTech/20131023/77597.html)

Words and Expressions

1.	petaflop	/ˈpetəflɒp/	n.	千万亿次
2.	quadrillion	/kwɒˈdrɪljən/	n	千的五次方,百万的四次方
3.	ongoing	/ˈɒŋɡəʊɪŋ/	adj.	不间断的
4.	microchip	/ˈmaɪkrəʊtʃɪp/	n.	微晶片
5.	execute	/ˈeksɪkjuːt/	vt.	执行
6.	predesigned	/priːdɪˈzaɪnd/	adj.	预先设定的
7.	microprocessor	/ˌmaɪkrəʊˈprəʊsesə(r)/	n.	微处理器
8.	node	/nəʊd/	n.	节点
9.	virtual	/ˈvɜːtʃuəl/	adj.	虚拟的
10.	scatter	/ˈskætə(r)/	vt.	分散
11.	simulate	/ˈsɪmjuleɪt/	vt.	模拟
12.	parallel machine			并行计算机
13.	cooling system			冷却系统
14	mathematical calculation			数学计算
15	down time			停机时间

Notes

1. Experts measured the supercomputer's performance at 33.86 petaflop or quadrillion of operations per second.

专家测到,该超级计算机的性能达到每秒33.86千万亿次运算。

2. China's National University of Defense Technology developed the supercomputer, which runs twice as fast as the No.2 rated Titan supercomputer.

中国国防科技大学研制了这台超级计算机,其运行速度是排名第二的泰坦超级计算机的两倍。

3. This Central Processing Unit, or CPU, executes a set of commands contained in a predesigned program.

这个被称为CPU的中央处理器执行预先设定程序中包含的一组控制命令。

4. Those are very easy to run on virtual supercomputers because each problem is independent of all the others and I can scatter these jobs out all around the place.

在虚拟超级计算机上运行那些很简单。因为每个问题都相互独立,我可以将这些工作分散到各个地方进行。

5. It's transforming science and engineering, and it's going to continue to transform it in ways I think most people don't fully grasp—how well we can model and simulate the world now.

这是在转换科学和工程,它还将用我认为多数人未能完全掌握的方法继续转换。这种方法就是现在我们可以多大程度地对世界进行建模和仿真。

Exercises

I. Structure Analysis

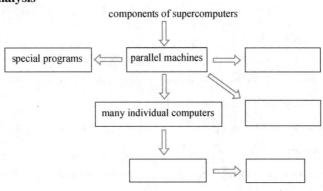

Ⅱ. Term Matching

Directions: Match the English terms with their Chinese equivalents.

1. cooling system   a. 停机时间
2. parallel machine   b. 数学计算
3. down time   c. 节点
4. mathematical calculation d. 微芯片
5. microchip   e. 冷却系统
6. node   f. 虚拟的
7. microprocessor   g. 执行
8. virtual   h. 并行计算机
9. execute   i. 千万亿次
10. petaflop   j. 微处理器

Ⅲ. Reading Comprehension

Directions: Choose the best answer to each of the following questions.

(   ) 1. How many CPUs does China's Tianhe-2 supercomputer have?
   A. One CPU.   B. A few more CPUs.
   C. Millions of CPUs.   D. Thousands of CPUs.

(   ) 2. What are the characters of parallel machines?
   A. They use a lot of power.   B. They create a lot of heat.
   C. They require huge cooling systems.   D. All of the above.

(   ) 3. How can a virtual supercomputer be created?
   A. It can be created by connection of a few computers within a university campus or company.
   B. It can be created by networking individual computers within a university campus or company.
   C. It can be created by connection of a few parallel machines within a university campus or company.
   D. It can be created by networking a few parallel machines within a university campus or company.

(   ) 4. Why is it easy to run on virtual supercomputers?
   A. Because each problem is independent of all the others and people can scatter those jobs out all around the place.
   B. Because virtual supercomputers can be created by anyone with enough resources.
   C. Because virtual supercomputers can process data during down time.

D. None of the above.

(　　) 5. What's Professor Grimshaw attitude toward supercomputers?

A. Doubtful.　　B. Pessimistic.　　C. Positive.　　D. Uncertain.

Text B

NFC Tags

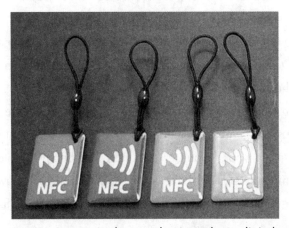

NFC **tags** are becoming increasingly popular in today's digital environment because they allow access to **a host of** information, quickly and easily. With these tags you can download information from film posters, read a **recipe** from an advertisement, select your university curriculum timetable and so much more.

It is predicted that one in five smartphones will include NFC by the year 2014. Contact-less payments are **at the forefront of** this new technology, and Barclays use a similar system for payments under £15 by allowing visa cards to be placed near the payment pad. Paying by phone, however, means that you can also receive **digital information** at the time of payment.

Some services such as "Find My iPhone" by Apple as well as HTC's Sense.com mean that if you lose your mobile phone, you can have it **wiped remotely** as soon as you notice it is missing. This **combats** some security issues regarding **instant** phone payments.

Because mobile phones have become such a necessary **accessory** in our lives, NFC phones are gaining steady popularity. A distribution of NFC phones is planned at the Olympic games this summer, with phones being distributed to athletes to raise awareness of this technology.

NFC phones also make sharing photos easier than ever. All you need to do is find the picture and tap the phone you want to pass it on to. Videos can also be shared instantly in the same way. Sharing business details and personal contacts can also be carried out by tapping phones together.

NFC is a completely wireless technology that enables data to be transferred between two devices. The data transferred can be text data or numbers. The tags themselves usually come in the form of **stickers** and contain tiny microchips that are able to transfer information to a mobile phone, as long as it is NFC enabled.

NFC tags (which are microchips) are locked so that any data stored on them cannot then be changed. Usually tags are not able to be unlocked again, making them more secure. Tags can be **encoded** by using an NFC-friendly mobile phone and then choosing the appropriate app to allow encoding to take place. Apps are also available that show your preferred weather page or turn your Wi-Fi on or off.

Soon everything and everyone could have a **digital signature**, making products, events, services, business and even people immediately accessible at the touch of a button. Imagine eating in your favourite restaurant and being able to touch your phone against the menu. Immediately you have all the dishes you love downloaded and ready for you to use whenever you want. NFC tags are making the digital future a reality. (446 words)

(http://www.nfctags.co.uk/index.php; http://www.nfctags.co.uk/nfc-phones.php)

Words and Expressions

1.	tag	/tæg/	n.	芯片；标签
2.	recipe	/ˈresəpi/	n.	食谱
3.	wipe	/waɪp/	v.	消除，抹去(计算机、磁带或录像带上的信息等)
4.	remotely	/rɪˈməʊtli/	adv.	遥远地
5.	combat	/ˈkɒmbæt/	vt.	防止
6.	instant	/ˈɪnstənt/	adj.	即时的
7.	accessory	/əkˈsesəri/	n.	配件
8.	sticker	/ˈstɪkə(r)/	n.	粘贴物
9.	encode	/ɪnˈkəʊd/	vt.	编码
10.	a host of			许多，大量

Unit 4　Electrical and Computer Engineering

11.	at the forefront of	处于最前列
12.	digital information	数字信息
13.	digital signature	数字签名

1. NFC（Near Field Communication）

近场通信，由飞利浦半导体（现恩智浦半导体公司）、诺基亚和索尼共同研制开发。是一种短距高频的无线电技术，在13.56MHz频率运行于20厘米距离内。NFC近场通信技术是由非接触式射频识别（RFID）及互联互通技术整合演变而来，在单一芯片上结合感应式读卡器、感应式卡片和点对点的功能，能在短距离内与兼容设备进行识别和数据交换。工作频率为13.56MHz。但是使用这种手机支付方案的用户必须更换特制的手机。目前这项技术在日韩被广泛应用。手机用户凭着配置了支付功能的手机就可以行遍全国：他们的手机可以用于机场登机验证以及用作大厦的门禁钥匙、交通一卡通、信用卡、支付卡等。

2. NFC tag

人们可以将一些个性化的功能写进去，用带有NFC功能的手机或者电脑，向NFC标签里面写数据。NFC标签的使用方法是将带有NFC芯片的手机通过扫描NFC标签，就可以立刻响应标签里的功能，比如最简单的开启飞行模式。另外，也可以写一个网址、电话号码进去，写好之后，当下次想打开这个网址或者拨写进去的电话号码的时候，只需将NFC标签和手机的NFC感应区贴一下，这个网址或者电话号码就会自动出现在手机上，非常方便。还有个用处是可以通过一些NFC软件，对NFC标签编程，就像是录制一样。

3. Contact-less payments are at the forefront of this new technology, and Barclays use a similar system for payments under £15 by allowing visa cards to be placed near the payment pad.

非接触式支付是这项新技术的前沿技术，巴克莱银行使用类似的支付系统允许签证置于附近的支付平板电脑上支付15英镑以下的金额。

4. Tags can be encoded by using an NFC-friendly mobile phone and then choosing the appropriate app to allow encoding to take place.

标签可以通过一个支持NFC的手机来对其编码，然后选择合适的应用程序来启动编码。

Exercises

I. **Reading Comprehension**

Directions: Judge whether each of the following statements is true(T) or false(F) according to the text, and correct the mistakes in the false statements.

(   ) 1. Barclays use the contact-less payment system for payments above £15 by allowing visa cards to be placed near the payment pad.

Modification:

(   ) 2. If you lose your mobile phone, you can use services such as "Find My iPhone" by Apple and have it wiped remotely as soon as you notice it is missing.

Modification:

(   ) 3. The data transferred only can be numbers between two devices.

Modification:

(   ) 4. Usually tags are able to be unlocked again.

Modification:

(   ) 5. Tags can be encoded by using an NFC-friendly mobile phone choosing the appropriate app to allow encoding to take place.

Modification:

II. **Questions for Discussion**

Directions: Answer the following questions with the information contained in Text B.

1. What do people do with NFC tags in daily life?
2. What's the benefit of some services such as "Find My iPhone" by Apple as well as HTC's Sense.com?
3. How to make NFC tags more secure?
4. What do you think of NFC tags?

Unit 5
Economics and Management

Text A

China's Money Outflow Not Investment Withdrawal: Authority

China's capital outflow last year should not **be equated with** withdrawal of foreign investment, **forex** administrant said on Thursday.

The outflow occurred as domestic banks and enterprises vigorously increased holdings of overseas assets and repaid debts, the State Administration of Foreign Exchange (SAFE) said when answering questions from reporters.

"There is an essential difference with the so-called withdrawal of foreign capital," the SAFE said.

In the first three quarters of last year, China's overseas assets increased by \$272.7 billion, and **deposits** in foreign banks and lending to foreign companies rose by \$96.9 billion, data showed.

China's overseas **net** financial assets **rank second** in the world, which inevitably prompts capital outflow as long as China maintains its current account **surplus**, the SAFE said.

By the end of 2015, China's **foreign exchange reserves shrank** to $3.3 trillion, but were still the world's largest.

China's huge reserve assets and stable external debt structure can provide strong resistance to impacts from **capital flows**, the SAFE said.

China's balance of international payments

China saw a capital account deficit in the fourth quarter of 2015 after a surplus registered in the previous quarter.

The deficit under the capital and financial account stood at $84.3 billion during the Sept-Dec period, reversing the surplus of $11.4 billion three months previous, according to preliminary statistics released by the SAFE.

In the meantime, **reserve assets**, most of which are foreign exchange, decreased by $115 billion, narrowing from a drop of $160 billion in the third quarter.

China started to post deficits on its capital and financial account in the second quarter of 2014 due to rapid increases in overseas investment and speculation on **depreciation** of *yuan*.

China reported a current account surplus of $84.3 billion in the fourth quarter, up from $60.3 billion posted in the third quarter.

For the whole of 2015, China saw a current account surplus at $293 billion, a capital and financial account deficit at $161 billion and a reserve assets drop at $343 billion. (352 words)

(http://www.chinadaily.com.cn/business/2016-02/05/content_23402314.htm)

Words and Expressions

1.	withdrawal	/wɪðˈdrɔːəl/	n.	移开；撤回，撤退
2.	forex	/ˈfɔːeks/	n.	[经]外汇
3.	deposit	/dɪˈpɒzɪt/	n.	储蓄，存款；保证金
4.	net	/net/	adj.	净的；净得的；最后的
5.	surplus	/ˈsɜːpləs/	n.	剩余额；顺差；盈余
6.	shrink	/ʃrɪŋk/	vi.	(经济)萎缩
7.	depreciation	/dɪˌpriːʃiˈeɪʃən/	n.	货币贬值；跌价；(资产等)折旧
8.	be equated with			等同于
9.	rank second			位列第二

10.	foreign exchange reserve	外汇储备
11.	capital flow	资本流动
12.	reserve asset	储备资产

Notes

1. the State Administration of Foreign Exchange (SAFE)

国家外汇管理局:是国务院部委管理的国家局,由中国人民银行管理,行政级别为副部级。内设 9 个职能司和机关党委,设置 4 个事业单位。在各省、自治区、直辖市、部分副省级城市设立 36 个分局(其中 2 个外汇管理部),在部分地(市)设立 308 个中心支局,在部分县(市)设立 519 个支局。国家外汇管理局分支机构与当地中国人民银行分支机构合署办公。其基本职能是:分析研究外汇收支和国际收支状况、监督管理外汇市场的运作秩序、经营管理国家外汇储备、依法检查境内机构执行外汇管理法规的情况,处罚违法违规行为。

2. China's overseas net financial assets rank second in the world, which inevitably prompts capital outflow as long as China maintains its current account surplus, the SAFE said.

国家外汇管理局说道:"中国的海外净金融资产在世界排名第二,只要中国保持当前账户余额就不可避免地促使资金外流。"

3. The deficit under the capital and financial account stood at $84.3 billion during the Sept-Dec period, reversing the surplus of $11.4 billion three months previous, according to preliminary statistics released by the SAFE.

根据国家外汇管理局发布的初步统计显示,资本和金融账户下的赤字在 9 月至 12 月期间为 843 亿美元,扭转了三个月之前 114 亿美元的余额。

4. China started to post deficits on its capital and financial account in the second quarter of 2014 due to rapid increases in overseas investment and speculation on depreciation of *yuan*.

由于海外投资的快速增加及对人民币贬值的猜想,中国在 2014 年第二季度开始显露在其资本和金融账户上的赤字。

Exercises

I. Structure Analysis

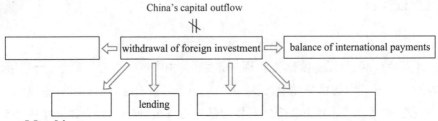

II. Term Matching

Directions: Match the English terms with their Chinese equivalents.

1. capital flow   a. 储蓄,存款；保证金
2. account surplus   b. 位列第二
3. the State Administration of Foreign Exchange (SAFE)   c. 纯利润
4. rank second   d. 资本流动
5. reserve asset   e. 国家外汇管理局
6. net profit   f. 不足额；赤字；亏损
7. foreign exchange reserve   g. 储备资产
8. depreciation   h. 外汇储备
9. deposit   i. 账户余额
10. deficit   j. 贬值；(资产等)折旧

III. Reading Comprehension

Directions: Choose the best answer to each of the following questions.

(　　) 1. Which of the following CANNOT be regarded as "China's money outflow"?
   A. Domestic banks increased holdings of overseas assets.
   B. Domestic banks increased holdings of repaid debts.
   C. Enterprises increased overseas assets.
   D. Enterprises increased domestic assets.

(　　) 2. During the January-September period, how much did China's foreign assets rise by?
   A. $96.9 billion.   B. $84.3 billion.
   C. $272.7 billion.   D. $11.4 billion.

(　　) 3. According to the SAFE, which of the following is TRUE?
   A. Domestic banks and enterprises vigorously increased holdings of overseas assets and repaid debts.

B. There is little difference between outflow and withdrawal of foreign capital.

C. China's overseas net financial assets are small.

D. China is not impacted from capital flows.

(　　) 4. From the third quarter to the fourth quarter, how much did the account surplus increase by?

　　A. $84.3 billion.　　　　B. $60.3 billion.

　　C. $24 billion.　　　　　D. $11.4 billion.

(　　) 5. By the end of 2015, what were China's foreign exchange reserves?

　　A. $293 billion.　　　　 B. $3.3 trillion.

　　C. $161 billion.　　　　 D. $343 billion.

Text B

How Mounting Job Cuts Could Threaten the UK's Economic Recovery

Major UK-based companies have announced tens of thousands of job losses that are expected to ripple through the economy in the coming months, **casting a shadow** over Britain's recovery.

Affecting vast areas of the UK economy—from factories to the high street, banking, media and energy—the job losses announced in the past fortnight **coincided with** another wave of panic selling on stock markets and fears of a further global **recession**.

The Organisation for Economic Cooperation and Development expressed concern on Thursday about the state of the global economy. It cut growth forecasts made three months ago and called on its members, including Britain, to ease up on **austerity**.

Two of the UK's biggest lenders, Lloyds Banking Group and Barclays, along with Credit Suisse, are **laying off** workers in the UK. BP and Shell have been prompted to cut jobs because of the **collapse** in **crude** prices, which has hit oil companies hard. And the

British gas owner, Centrica, **reiterate**d on Thursday that it is to **axe** 1,000 jobs in the UK this year, as part of 4,000 job cuts by 2020.

Michael Hewson, chief market analyst at CMC Markets UK, said, "These are all fairly highly paid roles ... You've got to think that over the next six months you're going to see some **trickle-down effect**. A lot of the recovery in the UK has been consumption-based, so that ultimately is going to hit consumption rates."

George Buckley, chief UK economist at Deutsche Bank, said the loss of highly paid city jobs, along with the new **stamp duty surcharge** on second homes from April, was likely to affect the **buy-to-let** market and the wider housing market. "We have a list of 10 reasons why we are nervous about London house prices," he said. "I imagine a lot of people who work in the financial services industry own buy-to-let property. It could have a knock-on effect on the buy-to-let market and the property market as a whole."

Lloyds Banking Group cut 1,755 jobs and close 29 branches.

The woes spread far and wide. Britain's steel industry, in which 5,000 workers have lost their jobs since last summer, has appealed to the government for emergency assistance. Tata, which owns the **remnants** of British steel, announced 1,050 job cuts last month.

Frances O'Grady, general secretary of the Trades Union Congress, said, "The UK labour market is becoming more **polarised** by the day. The loss of important middle-income jobs, in industries such as steel, should concern us all."

Weak wage growth is also a problem. Wages excluding bonuses had risen by 2% year-on-year at the end of 2015—half the pre-crisis average of about 4%, according to the latest official figures published on Wednesday. (462 words)

(http://www.theguardian.com/business/2016/feb/18/how-mounting-job-cuts-could-threaten-uks-economic-recovery)

Words and Expressions

1.	cast	/ˈkɑːst/	vt.	投射
2.	recession	/rɪˈseʃən/	n.	经济衰退,不景气
3.	austerity	/ɒˈsterəti/	n.	简朴,朴素;节衣缩食
4.	collapse	/kəˈlæps/	n.	(突然)降价,贬值;暴跌
5.	crude	/kruːd/	n.	原油
6.	reiterate	/riˈɪtəreɪt/	vt.	重申;反复地说
7.	axe	/æks/	vt.	大量削减

8.	remnant	/ˈremnənt/	n.	剩余部分
9.	polarize	/ˈpəʊləraɪz/	vt.	使两极化
10.	cast a shadow			蒙上一层阴影
11.	coincide with			与……一致,与……相符
12.	lay off			暂时解雇,裁员
13.	trickle-down effect			涓滴效应
14.	stamp duty surcharge			印花税票
15.	buy-to-let			购房出租

 Notes

1. the Organisation for Economic Cooperation and Development

经济合作与发展组织,简称经合组织(OECD),是由34个市场经济国家组成的政府间国际经济组织,旨在共同应对全球化带来的经济、社会和政府治理等方面的挑战,并把握全球化带来的机遇。该组织成立于1961年,目前成员国总数34个,总部设在巴黎。

2. Two of the UK's biggest lenders, Lloyds Banking Group and Barclays, along with Credit Suisse, are laying off workers in the UK. BP and Shell have been prompted to cut jobs because of the collapse in crude prices, which has hit oil companies hard. And the British Gas owner, Centrica, reiterated on Thursday that it is to axe 1,000 jobs in the UK this year, as part of 4,000 job cuts by 2020.

英国两个最大的贷款方,劳埃德银行集团和巴克莱银行以及瑞士信贷,在英国正在裁员。英国石油和贝壳石油公司由于原油价格暴跌一直被催促要裁员,这严重地打击了石油公司。英国燃气公司森特理克在周四重申,今年在英国将裁员1000人,达到2020年4000人的一部分。

3. trickle-down effect

涓滴效应,又译作渗漏效应、滴漏效应、滴入论、垂滴说,也称作"涓滴理论"(利益均沾论、渗漏理论、滴漏理论),指在经济发展过程中并不给予贫困阶层、弱势群体或贫困地区特别的优待,而是由优先发展起来的群体或地区通过消费、就业等方面惠及贫困阶层或地区,带动其发展和富裕,或认为政府财政津贴可经过大企业再陆续流入小企业和消费者之手,从而更好地促进经济增长的理论。

4. The woes spread far and wide. Britain's steel industry, in which 5,000 workers have lost their jobs since last summer, has appealed to the government for emergency assistance. Tata, which owns the remnants of British steel, announced 1,050 job cuts last month.

恶事传千里。英国的钢铁行业已呼吁政府紧急援助，它自去年夏天以来已有5000名员工失去了工作。拥有英国残余钢铁的塔塔集团上月宣布裁员1050人。

5. Frances O'Grady, general secretary of the Trades Union Congress, said, "The UK labour market is becoming more polarised by the day. The loss of important middle-income jobs, in industries such as steel, should concern us all."

英国工会联盟总秘书长弗朗西斯·奥格雷迪说："英国劳动力市场正变得日益两极分化。失去诸如钢铁行业重要的中等收入的工作会让我们所有人担心。"

Exercises

I. Reading Comprehension

Directions: Judge whether each of the following statements is true (T) or false (F) according to the text, and correct the mistakes in the false statements.

(   ) 1. The Organisation for Economic Cooperation and Development worried about the state of the global economy.

Modification:

(   ) 2. Lloyds Banking Group and Barclays, along with Credit Suisse, are laying off workers in the USA.

Modification:

(   ) 3. The British gas owner, Centrica, reiterated on Thursday that it is to add 1,000 jobs in the UK this year.

Modification:

(   ) 4. According to Michael Hewson, consumption rates will not be affected by the recovery in the UK.

Modification:

(   ) 5. Wages had risen by 2% year-on-year at the end of 2015.

Modification:

II. Questions for Discussion

Directions: Answer the following questions with the information contained in Text B.

1. Which areas of the UK economy can be affected by job losses?
2. Why have BP and Shell been prompted to cut jobs?
3. According to George Buckley, what are the results of the loss of highly-paid city jobs?
4. What's the relationship between job losses and the economy?

Unit 6
Food and Chemical Engineering

Text A

Secret Air Pollutants in Our Homes Claim Thousands of Lives

Thousands more people than previously thought are dying each year from the effect of poor air quality, including pollutants from everyday objects and appliances in their homes. At least 40,000 deaths a year can be linked to the effect of air pollution, with thousands more deaths across Europe. But while the danger of outdoor air pollution has been well documented in recent years, more dangers are from the secret killers in our homes.

It will warn that everyday kitchen products, faulty boilers, **open fires**, **fly sprays** and even **air fresheners**, contribute to poor indoor air quality. The danger of potentially fatal **carbon monoxide** from faulty boilers and heaters, along with **particulates** and **nitrogen oxides** from heating and cooking appliances can damage the lungs and the heart.

But the most disturbing aspects of air pollution are posed by such common items as air fresheners and personal **hygiene**, DIY and cleaning products. These often use chemicals known as **volatile organic compounds** (**VOCs**), which start off as solids or liquids but readily evaporate into the air. Furthermore, certain furniture, fabric, furnishings, glue and insulation can emit **formaldehyde** vapour, causing irritation to the lungs. Biological materials found in the home, such as house-dust **mites**, **mould** and animal **dander**—**flecks** of skin and fur—can also harm human health.

While young children and the elderly are particularly sensitive to air pollution, it can have an adverse impact across our entire lifespan. Examples include the adverse effects of air pollution on the development of the **foetus**, including lung and kidney development, and **miscarriage**; increases in heart attacks and **strokes** for those in later life; and the associated links to **asthma**, **diabetes**, **dementia**, **obesity** and cancer for the wider population.

More should be done to **crack down** on polluters and protect the public from harmful emissions, particularly in urban areas and close to schools. Local authorities should be given the power to close or divert roads to reduce the volume of traffic, especially near schools, when pollution levels are high. It also wants tougher legislation to force polluters to reduce their harmful emissions. (342 words)

(http://www.telegraph.co.uk)

Words and Expressions

1.	particulate	/pɑːˈtɪkjələt/	n.	微粒
2.	hygiene	/ˈhaɪdʒiːn/	n.	卫生
3.	formaldehyde	/fɔːˈmældɪhaɪd/	n.	甲醛
4.	mite	/maɪt/	n.	螨虫
5.	mould	/məʊld/	n.	霉
6.	dander	/ˈdændə/	n.	皮屑
7.	fleck	/flek/	n.	微粒,斑点
8.	foetus	/ˈfiːtəs/	n.	胎儿
9.	miscarriage	/ˈmɪskærɪdʒ/	n.	流产,早产
10.	stroke	/strəʊk/	n.	中风
11.	asthma	/ˈæsmə/	n.	哮喘
12.	diabetes	/ˌdaɪəˈbiːtiːz/	n.	糖尿病
13.	dementia	/dɪˈmenʃə/	n.	痴呆
14.	obesity	/əʊˈbiːsətɪ/	n.	肥胖症
15.	open fire			明火

16.	fly spray	蚊虫喷雾剂
17.	air freshener	空气清新剂
18.	carbon monoxide	一氧化碳
19.	nitrogen oxide	氮氧化合物
20.	volatile organic compounds (VOCs)	挥发性有机物
21.	crack down	采取严厉措施，镇压

 Notes

1. It will warn that everyday kitchen products, faulty boilers, open fires, fly sprays and even air fresheners, contribute to poor indoor air quality.

这将警示人们日常使用的厨房用品、有损坏的锅炉、明火、蚊虫喷雾剂，甚至是空气清新剂，都会导致室内空气质量不良。

2. The danger of potentially fatal carbon monoxide from faulty boilers and heaters, along with particulates and nitrogen oxides from heating and cooking appliances can damage the lungs and the heart.

由破损锅炉、取暖器散发的潜在致命一氧化碳，以及加热及烹饪用具所产生的微粒和氮氧化合物都会给人体肺部及心脏带来伤害。

3. Furthermore, certain furniture, fabric, furnishings, glue and insulation can emit formaldehyde vapour, causing irritation to the lungs.

另外，某些家具、织物、摆设、胶水、绝缘体都会释放甲醛气体，刺激肺部。

4. Biological materials found in the home, such as house-dust mites, mould and animal dander—flecks of skin and fur—can also harm human health.

在家中发现的生物，如家庭尘螨、霉、动物皮屑——皮肤及毛发的微粒——也会对人体健康造成伤害。

Unit 6 Food and Chemical Engineering

Exercises

I. Structure Analysis

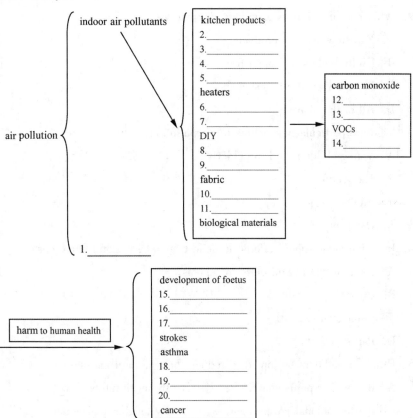

II. Term Matching

Directions: Match the English terms with their Chinese equivalents.

1. open fire
2. air freshener
3. volatile organic compounds (VOCs)
4. fly sprays
5. carbon monoxide
6. diabetes
7. formaldehyde
8. obesity
9. mite
10. nitrogen oxide

a. 挥发性有机物
b. 糖尿病
c. 甲醛
d. 明火
e. 空气清新剂
f. 蚊虫喷雾剂
g. 一氧化碳
h. 螨虫
i. 氮氧化合物
j. 肥胖症

Ⅲ. **Reading Comprehension**

Directions: Choose the best answer to each of the following questions.

(   ) 1. According to Para. 1, where are more dangers of air pollution from?

    A. Outdoor pollutants.   B. Everyday objects and appliances in the homes.

    C. Europe.   D. Pollutants from factories.

(   ) 2. What contributes to poor indoor air quality?

    A. Everyday kitchen products.

    B. Faulty boilers and open fires.

    C. Fly sprays and air fresheners.

    D. All of the above.

(   ) 3. Who are particularly sensitive to air pollution?

    A. Young children and the elderly.

    B. The foetus.

    C. Adults.

    D. Old people.

(   ) 4. In which areas should efforts be done to reduce harmful emissions?

    A. Areas in urban and close to schools.

    B. Homes.

    C. Outdoor areas.

    D. Parks.

(   ) 5. How can polluters be forced to reduce their harmful emissions?

    A. By tougher punishment.   B. By local authorities.

    C. By the national government.   D. By tougher legislation.

Text B

Norwegian Confectioner Improves Safety and Efficiency

Norway's leading supplier of candy, Nidar AS, built in 1950, the company's plant has been periodically updated with newer **bulk** handling equipment to improve productivity and working conditions. But due to the building's design, the space presents challenges for the company.

Tight places make gravity feeding of materials impossible in some sections of the plant. In these areas, bulk materials are transferred using bulk bag **dischargers**, flexible

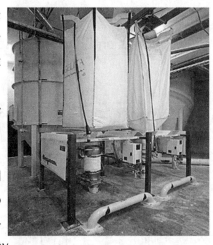

screw conveyors, **rigid augers** and **pneumatic** conveyors. These pieces of equipment not only reduce manual labor and contain dust, they also fit in the allotted space.

The newest bulk bag discharger is a twin **half-frame** unit that handles two types of **starch** in a small space on the plant's fourth floor. Previously, operators carried 55 **lb**. bags of starch from the third to the fourth floor where it was **dumped into** two large vessels, each holding 440 to 660 lb. Thirty-two bags were handled manually each eight-hour day.

The starch powder flowed by gravity from two large vessels through a pair of knife gate **valves** and 6-in. diameter steel **chutes**. The large vessels could not be replaced with two separate bulk bag dischargers because the distance between the discharger outlets would have exceeded the distance between the existing chutes. Also, the ceiling is less than 15 ft. high, which does not provide enough headroom above the units to use a **forklift** for loading and removing bulk bags.

To surmount both problems, a 4 ft. high, twin half-frame bulk bag discharger was installed. The unit discharges through two outlets spaced closely enough to avoid relocating the knife gate valves and chutes, while the low **profile** design allows suspension of bulk bags from a hoist, saving 4 in. of headroom. The discharger holds two bulk bags side-by-side that provide enough starch to keep the line running for two or more days.

Once a bag is hoisted into position, an operator pulls the bag spout over a **clamp** ring to create a secure, dust-tight connection between the clean side of the bag spout and the clean side of a **telescoping tube**. As the bag empties and **elongates**, the telescoping tube maintains constant downward tension, promoting complete discharge. Additional support of flow through the spout is provided by the bag **activators** that raise opposite bottom sides of the bag into a steep "V" shape.

After descending through the telescoping tube, the starch passes through the knife gate valve and then through one of the two **vertical** chutes to a weighing station on the second floor. A horizontally oriented 6.7-in. diameter auger on the third floor can run in either direction, so each discharger can supply either of the two weighing stations that send the signals to open or close the knife gate valves. (463 words)

(http://www.foodengineeringmag.com)

Words and Expressions

1.	bulk	/bʌlk/	n.	体积;大块
2.	discharger	/dɪsˈtʃɑːdʒə/	n.	卸货人
3.	screw	/skruː/	n.	螺丝钉;螺旋桨
4.	pneumatic	/njuːˈmætɪk/	adj.	充气的;气动的
5.	starch	/stɑːtʃ/	n.	淀粉,含淀粉的食物
6.	lb		abbr.	磅
7.	valve	/vælv/	n.	阀,真空管
8.	chute	/ʃuːt/	n.	斜槽,滑道
9.	forklift	/ˈfɔːklɪft/	n.	铲车,叉式升降机
10	profile	/ˈprəʊfaɪl/	n.	侧面,半面;外形,轮廓
11.	clamp	/klæmp/	n.	钳,压板
12.	elongate	/ˈiːlɒŋgeɪt/	v.	延长,加长
13.	activator	/ˈæktɪveɪtə/	n.	催化剂,触媒剂
14.	vertical	/ˈvɜːtɪkl/	adj.	垂直的,竖立的
15.	rigid auger			刚性钻
16.	half-frame			半幅,半框
17.	dump into			倒入
18.	telescoping tube			伸缩管

 ## Notes

1. Nidar AS

挪威零售集团奥克拉集团的子公司,是糕点糖果的生产商和经销商,公司位于特隆赫姆市。公司成立于1912年,是挪威最主要的糖果公司之一。

2. In these areas, bulk materials are transferred using bulk bag dischargers, flexible screw conveyors, rigid augers and pneumatic conveyors.

在这些区域,使用大型袋式卸货机、活动螺旋传输机、刚性钻和气动传输机来传输大型物资。

3. The newest bulk bag discharger is a twin half-frame unit that handles two types of starch in a small space on the plant's fourth floor.

最新的大型袋式卸货机是一种带有两个半副袋子的装置,可同时处理两种淀粉,占用空间小,位于公司的四楼。

4. The starch powder flowed by gravity from two large vessels through a pair of

knife gate valves and 6-in. diameter steel chutes.

由于重力,淀粉通过一对刀型进模口阀门和直径为 6 英寸的钢制斜槽,从两个大型容器中流出。

5. As the bag empties and elongates, the telescoping tube maintains constant downward tension, promoting complete discharge.

随着袋子倒空拉伸,伸缩管维持持续向下的拉力,完成卸货。

Exercises

Ⅰ. Reading Comprehension

Directions: Judge whether each of the following statements is true(T) or false(F) according to the text, and correct the mistakes in the false statements.

(　　) 1. The company doesn't have enough space to transfer some materials.
Modification:

(　　) 2. The equipment is high in labor efficiency and is environment-friendly.
Modification:

(　　) 3. Previously operators handled 32 bags manually each day.
Modification:

(　　) 4. There was not enough headroom to equip the bulk bags previously.
Modification:

(　　) 5. In order to install the bulk bag dischargers, the knife gate valves and chutes need to be relocated.
Modification:

Ⅱ. Questions for Discussion

Directions: Answer the following questions with the information contained in Text B.

1. Why does the company update the handling equipment and install the bulk bag dischargers?
2. How do the newest bulk bag dischargeres work?
3. What is the difference between the previous bulk bag discharger and the newest one?
4. How do you think about the newest bulk bag dischargers?

Unit 7

Art and Design

Text A

Michelangelo

Michelangelo was a painter, **sculptor**, architect and poet and one of the great artists of the Italian **Renaissance**.

Michelangelo Buonarroti was born on 6 March, 1475 in Caprese near Florence (Italy) where his father was the local **magistrate**. A few weeks after his birth, the family moved to Florence. In 1488, Michelangelo was apprenticed to the painter Domenico Ghirlandaio. He then lived in the household of Lorenzo de' Medici, the leading **patron** of the arts in Florence.

After the Medici were expelled from Florence, Michelangelo travelled to Bologna and then, in 1496, to Rome. His primary works were **sculptures** in these early years.

Engraved Portrait of Michelangelo (1475 – 1564)

Michelangelo was an old, sick man when he began **carving** a sculpture known as *The Florence pietà* (a pietà is a sculpture of the **Virgin Mary** holding the dead body of Jesus). He worked on the sculpture only at night, and sometimes was in such pain that he could not work at all. In describing the sculpture, Michelangelo's biographer wrote of its great "beauty and sorrow". His *Pietà* (1497) made his name and he returned to Florence a famous sculptor. Here he produced his *David* (1501 –1504).

In 1505, Pope Julius Ⅱ **summoned** Michelangelo back to Rome and **commissioned** him to design Julius' own tomb. Due to quarrels between Julius and Michelangelo, and many other demands on the artist's time, the project was never completed, although

Michelangelo did produce a sculpture of **Moses** for the tomb.

Michelangelo's next major commission was the **fresco** in the **Sistine Chapel** in the **Vatican** (1508 –1512). It was recognized at once as a great work of art and from then on Michelangelo was regarded as Italy's greatest living artist.

The new **pope**, Leo X, then commissioned Michelangelo to rebuild the **facade** of the church of San Lorenzo in Florence and to adorn it with sculptures. The scheme was eventually abandoned, but it marks the beginning of Michelangelo's activity as an architect. Michelangelo also designed **monuments** to Giuliano and Lorenzo de' Medici in the **Medici Chapel** in San Lorenzo.

In 1534, Michelangelo returned to Rome where he was commissioned to paint ***The Last Judgment*** on the **altar** wall of the Sistine Chapel (1537 –1541). The fresco depicts the second coming of Christ and his judgment of the souls. From 1546 he was increasingly active as an architect, in particular on the great **Church of St Peter's**.

He died in Rome on 18 February, 1564. He left numberless unsurpassable works of art to the world. (409 words)

(http://www.bbc.co.uk/history/historic_figures/michelangelo.shtml)

Words and Expressions

1.	sculptor	/ˈskʌlptə(r)/	n.	雕刻家,雕塑家
2.	Renaissance	/rɪˈneɪsns/	n.	文艺复兴;文艺复兴时期
3.	magistrate	/ˈmædʒɪstreɪt/	n.	地方法官,治安官;文职官员
4.	patron	/ˈpeɪtrən/	n.	赞助人,资助人
5.	sculpture	/ˈskʌlptʃə(r)/	n.	雕刻术;塑像;雕刻品
6.	carve	/kɑːv/	vt.	切开;雕刻
7.	pietà	/pjeɪˈtɑː/	n.	圣母怜子图,圣母怜子像(雕刻)
8.	Virgin Mary		n.	圣母玛利亚(耶稣基督之母)
9.	summon	/ˈsʌmən/	vt.	传唤,召唤
10.	commission	/kəˈmɪʃn/	vt.	任命;正式委托
11.	Moses	/ˈməʊzɪz/	n.	摩西(《圣经》故事中犹太人的古代领袖)
12.	fresco	/ˈfreskəʊ/	n.	壁画
13.	Vatican	/ˈvætɪkən/	n.	梵蒂冈
14.	pope	/pəʊp/	n.	(罗马天主教的)教皇

15.	facade	/fəˈsɑːd/	n.	(尤指大型建筑物的)正面,临街的一面
16.	monument	/ˈmɒnjumənt/	n.	纪念碑;遗迹;遗址;丰碑
17.	altar	/ˈɔːltə(r)/	n.	祭坛,圣坛;圣餐台
18.	Sistine Chapel		n.	(罗马梵蒂冈的)西斯廷教堂
19.	Medici Chapel		n.	美第奇教堂
20.	*The Last Judgment*			《末日审判》(画)
21.	Church of St Peter's			圣彼得教堂

 Notes

1. He then lived in the household of Lorenzo de' Medici, the leading patron of the arts in Florence.

他住在洛伦佐·德·美第奇家里,洛伦佐·德·美第奇是当时佛罗伦萨主要的艺术赞助人。

2. Michelangelo was an old, sick man when he began carving a sculpture known as *The Florence Pietà*(a pietà is a sculpture of the Virgin Mary holding the dead body of Jesus).

米开朗琪罗开始雕刻佛罗伦萨的《哀悼基督》(《哀悼基督》是圣母玛丽亚抱着死去的耶稣的雕塑)时年老体衰。

3. Michelangelo's next major commission was the fresco in the Sistine Chapel in the Vatican (1508 –1512).

米开朗琪罗的下一个主要任务是完成梵蒂冈西斯廷教堂的壁画(1508—1512)。原来西斯廷教堂的穹顶绘有天空图案的壁画。1506 年,教皇朱理二世为了纪念叔父西克斯图斯四世,命米开朗琪罗重新绘制穹顶壁画。米开朗琪罗独自一人于 1508 年开始设计创作此壁画,并命名为《创世纪》。而西斯廷教堂也因拥有了米开朗琪罗最有代表性的两大巨制壁画《创世纪》和《最后的审判》而闻名于天下。

4. The new pope, Leo X, then commissioned Michelangelo to rebuild the facade of the church of San Lorenzo in Florence and to adorn it with sculptures.

新教皇利奥十世然后任命米开朗琪罗重建佛罗伦萨圣洛伦佐教堂的门面并刻上雕像作为装饰。

5. *The Last Judgment* on the altar wall of the Sistine Chapel

西斯廷教堂神坛壁画《末日审判》。新的教皇保罗三世要求他在神坛后的墙壁上作画。他辛勤地工作了 7 年,终于在 1541 完成了这部著作《末日审判》。这幅祭坛画高

14.6米,宽13.4米,描绘了耶稣基督审判众生灵魂的情景。

Exercises

I. Structure Analysis

The Profile of Michelangelo

Michelangelo was a great artist of the Italian Renaissance.

1475 – 1496

Michelangelo began his career as a(n) 1._____ in these early years.

1497 – 1507

Michelangelo made his name with 2._____.

He did not complete Julius' commission to 3._____ but he produced 4._____ for the tomb.

1508 – 1533

Michelangelo's major commission in this period was 5._____ in the Vatican, which made him regarded as Italy's greatest living 6._____.

1534 – 1564

In 1534, Michelangelo was commissioned to paint 7._____ on the 8._____ wall of the Sistine Chapel.

Michelangelo died at the age of 9._____, with 10._____ left behind the world.

David

II. Term Matching

Directions: Match the English terms with their Chinese equivalents.

1. painter   a. 雕塑
2. sculptor   b. 建筑家
3. architect   c. 雕塑家
4. sculpture   d. 西斯庭教堂壁画
5. fresco in the Sistine Chapel   e. 《末日审判》
6. facade   f. 圣母怜子图,圣母怜子像(雕像)
7. *The Last Judgment*   g. 正面
8. design   h. 画家
9. monument   i. 设计
10. pietà   j. 纪念碑

III. Reading Comprehension

Directions: Choose the best answer to each of the following questions.

(　　) 1. What is TRUE about Michelangelo's early life?

　　A. He was a magistrate.

　　B. He got help from Lorenzo de' Medici.

　　C. He was born in Florence.

　　D. He was a patron to many artists.

(　　) 2. What were Michelangelo's major works in his early years?

　　A. Painting.　　B. Architecture.　　C. Sculpture.　　D. Poetry.

(　　) 3. What is the impact of *The Florence Pietà* on Michelangelo?

　　A. It brought him fame.

　　B. It made him happy and healthy.

　　C. It made him escape to Florence.

　　D. He could not work at all after it was finished.

(　　) 4. Which is one of the reasons for the incompletion of the project of Julius' tomb?

　　A. Because of Michelangelo's laziness.

　　B. Because Julius cancelled the plan.

　　C. Because Michelangelo did not like the sculpture any more.

　　D. Because of the conflict between the artist and the pope.

(　　) 5. What did Michelangelo NOT do for the Sistine Chapel?

　　A. He painted *The Last Judgment*.　　B. He painted a pietà there.

　　C. He carved its ceiling.　　D. A and C.

Text B

Chanel

Some people think luxury is the opposite of poverty. It is not. It is the opposite of vulgarity.

—Coco Chanel

Since Chanel introduced the "little black dress" (LBD) in 1926, it has become the **epitome** of **chic**. Her first LBD was a **slash-necked**, short silk dress with only **diagonal pin tucks** as decoration. American *Vogue* called it the "Ford". Like Henry Ford's Model-T car, the LBD was an instant hit, widely available, though only in black. Chanel

believed fashion should be functional as well as chic. Radically simple, her LBD was designed not to show **stains** and to fit every woman. It was meant as the fashion ideal: a perfectly simple, yet sexy object.

To modern eyes, Chanel's original LDB may seem rather plain, perhaps too simple, at least compared to the **glamorous Givenchy** LDB (above) worn by Audrey Hepburn in the 1954 film *Sabrina* (Paramount Pictures). Until she was seventeen in 1900, Gabrielle Chanel was educated at a **convent orphanage** run by nuns. It does not take a psychologist to see in Chanel's revolutionary LBD concept a subconscious **affinity** for the "uniform" (the nun's habit) worn by the women who had raised the penniless **provincial** girl.

As early as 1915, Coco Chanel **envisioned** the LDB as the new uniform for women for afternoon and evening wear. Though apparently quite simple, these dresses showed **masterful** cut and proportion. She used traditional elegant materials like lace, tulle, and soft weightless silks in a newly tailored way. The LBD made women wearing anything else seem **overdressed**.

One time at an opera gala, Chanel saw many women in Paul Poiret's clothes with brilliant, **clashing** colors. From that day Chanel, the champion of **beige** and **neutrals**, was determined to change the fashion landscape. She rejected the accusation that she was trying to impose the style of the working girl on **haute couture** by creating the "**de luxe** poor look".

By the end of the 1920s, Chanel had triumphed. Although never a brilliant designer, she was a fashion **visionary**, who could intuit the needs and desires of stylish women. Chanel was the first **couturier** to understand the most profound fashion change of the century—in the clothes she wore daily, a woman no longer had to create the impression of great wealth. *Vogue* summed up the designer's impact: "Chanel's **silhouette**, begins to make the skirts of Lanvin look old-fashioned and Poiret too theatrical."

Paul Poiret, the king of fashing before WWI, spent his final years in decline and debt, having been surpassed by modernist designers like Coco Chanel. She and Poiret had a chance to encounter on a Paris street in 1928. Noticing that Chanel was wearing all black, Poiret inquired, "For whom, Madame, do you **mourn**?" To which Chanel replied, "For you, **Monsieur**." (445 words)

(https://www.vintagetextile.com/little_black_dress.htm)

Words and Expressions

1.	epitome	/ɪˈpɪtəmi/	n.	典型；典范
2.	chic	/ʃiːk/	n.	高雅，雅致
3.	slash-necked	/ˈslæʃˌnekt/	adj.	斜线颈的
4.	diagonal	/daɪˈægənl/	adj.	斜线的；斜的；斜纹的
5.	pin tuck	/ˈpɪnˈtʌk/	n.	细缝儿，细褶儿
6.	stain	/steɪn/	n.	污迹；污渍
7.	glamorous	/ˈglæmərəs/	adj.	富有魅力的；迷人的
8.	Givenchy	/dʒɪˈvɑnʃɪ/	n.	纪梵希（法国时装品牌）
9.	convent	/ˈkɒnvənt/	n.	女修道院
10.	orphanage	/ˈɔːfənɪdʒ/	n.	孤儿院；孤儿身份
11.	affinity	/əˈfɪnəti/	n.	密切关系
12.	provincial	/prəˈvɪnʃl/	adj.	乡下的；外地人的；粗野的
13.	envision	/ɪnˈvɪʒn/	vt.	想象，预见，展望
14.	masterful	/ˈmɑːstəfl/	adj.	熟练的；娴熟的
15.	overdressed	/ˌəʊvəˈdrest/	adj.	穿着过于正经的，打扮过度的
16.	clashing	/ˈklæʃɪŋ/	adj.	不相容的，相冲突的
17.	beige	/beɪʒ/	n.	米黄色；淡棕色
18.	neutral	/ˈnjuːtrəl/	n.	素净色
19.	haute couture	/ˌəʊt kuˈtjʊə(r)/	n.	高级女式时装
20.	de luxe	/ˌdəˈlʌks/	adj.	高级的；豪华的
21.	visionary	/ˈvɪʒənri/	n.	有远见的人，有智慧的人
22.	couturier	/kuˈtjʊərieɪ/	n.	女裁缝师，女服设计师
23.	silhouette	/ˌsɪluˈet/	n.	（服装）轮廓
24.	mourn	/mɔːn/	vi.	哀悼；哀痛
25.	Monsieur	/məˈsjɜː/	n.	先生（对法国男性的尊称）

Notes

1. American *Vogue* called it the "Ford". Like Henry Ford's Model-T car, the LBD was an instant hit, widely available, though only in black.

美国版《时尚》杂志更是将香奈儿的小黑裙称为"香奈儿的福特"。和亨利·福特设计的T型车一样,小黑裙立刻走进了千家万户,虽然它仅有黑色。(Model-T,即福特T型车,是福特汽车公司于1908年至1927年推出的一款汽车产品,车身黑色,广为流行。)

2. It does not take a psychologist to see in Chanel's revolutionary LBD concept a subconscious affinity for the "uniform" (the nun's habit) worn by the women who had raised the penniless provincial girl.

即使不是心理学家,也能看出香奈儿史无前例的小黑裙和她潜意识里对修女们的黑色制服(修女裙)的怀念有密切关系——正是她们将这个身无分文的村野女孩养育成人。

3. Though apparently quite simple, these dresses showed masterful cut and proportion. She used traditional elegant materials like lace, tulle, and soft weightless silks in a newly tailored way.

虽然看起来很简单,这些小黑裙裁剪精湛,比例协调。她(香奈儿)选择蕾丝、薄纱及轻软飘逸的丝绸等传统的优雅布料,以全新的方式进行裁剪。

4. *Vogue* summed up the designer's impact: "Chanel's silhouette, begins to make the skirts of Lanvin look old-fashioned and Poiret too theatrical."

《时尚》杂志总结了设计师的影响:"香奈儿服装的线条,开始让浪凡的裙子显得过时,而普瓦雷的设计又显夸张了。"

5. She and Poiret had a chance to encounter on a Paris street in 1928. Noticing that Chanel was wearing all black, Poiret inquired, "For whom, Madame, do you mourn?" To which Chanel replied, "For you, Monsieur."

1928年的一天,香奈儿和普瓦雷在巴黎街头偶遇。看到香奈儿一身黑色,普瓦雷问:"小姐,你在为谁默哀?"香奈儿回答:"为你,亲爱的先生。"

Exercises

Ⅰ. **Reading Comprehension**

Directions: Judge whether each of the following statements is true(T) or false(F) according to the text, and correct the mistakes in the false statements.

(   ) 1. Chanel's LBD had many decorations and was rather luxurious.
Modification:

(   ) 2. Chanel's LBD designed for Audrey Hepburn was glamorous and classic.
Modification:

(　　) 3. Chanel's LBD became women's new uniform for the parties.
Modification:

(　　) 4. Chanel followed Poiret's fashion ideal and used many colors in her clothes.
Modification:

(　　) 5. Chanel was sensitive to fashion and knew what stylish women liked.
Modification:

Ⅱ. Questions for Discussion

Directions: Answer the following questions with the information contained in Text B.

1. What is the fashion ideal of Chanel's LBD?

2. Can you sum up the characteristics of Chanel's LBD?

3. What's the most profound fashion change in the early 20th century according to the passage?

4. What's your opinion on Coco Chanel's career in fashion?

应用文写作

Unit 1 Manual

一、英文说明书及其常用模板

英文说明书是使用英文写的说明书,是产品生产者向消费者清晰、全面地介绍产品的文字材料,包括介绍产品的名称、用途、性能、生产日期、构造、配方、使用方法、生产日期、有限期、保养维护、注意事项等,语言准确明了。说明书具有三大功能:介绍产品,指导消费,扩大销售。

英文说明书具有以下几个语言特点:

1. 语言准确无误,尤其是涉及数字及日期的时候,一定要确保准确。如:Shelf life: Twelve months (to be kept under the temperature of −18 ℃). 保质期:−18℃以下温度保存12个月。

2. 表达简洁明晰。说明书的一个重要作用在于指导消费者,为了给消费者提供明确、清晰的指示,语言表达必须简洁清晰,不能模棱两可,不能太冗长拖沓,影响消费者的理解。如:The tablets have sugar coatings. When the coatings are removed, they appear brown with light, sweet and bitter taste. 本品为糖衣片,除去糖衣后,显棕褐色,味甘,微苦。

3. 常用名词或名词化结构。英文说明书是典型的科技文本,语言客观、结构严谨,因此在英文说明书中常常使用名词化结构。如:Unfamiliarity with the equipment, poor fault judgment or lack of proper training may cause injury to both the operator and others. 不熟悉设备,判断故障不当,或缺乏正确的培训,都可能会给操作者本人和他人造成伤害。

4. 使用术语。英文说明书是典型的科技文本,专业性强,常使用技术性表达。以下便是对比:

说明书常用词汇(短语)	日常生活常用词汇(短语)	中文含义
application	use	应用
construction	structure, building	结构,建造
commission	experiment and adjustment	调试
hazard	danger	危险
prior to	before	之前
terminate	end	结束,终止

5. 常使用缩略词。

说明书缩略词	完整词	中文含义
AC	alternating current	交流电
ad.	adjustment	调节
cal	calibration	校准
I/O	input/output	输入和输出
max	maximum	最大
temp.	temperature	温度

6. 多使用一般现在时态。说明书描述的是一般事实，故常使用一般现在时。如：Eye shadow applies smoothly and even with the new velvety formula, provides an unforgettable look with eye-opening colors and lightweight feel. 明媚的色彩，上妆柔滑细腻，令美目顾盼生辉。

7. 多使用祈使句和主动语态，这是由于说明书的指示功能。如：Read and follow warnings and instructions supplied by the battery manufacturer. 阅读并遵循电池制造商提供的所有警告和说明。

在书写英文说明书时，要特别注意这些语言特点，才能写出符合规范的文本。

说明书的结构通常由标题、正文、落款三个部分构成。标题一般要说明产品的名称、型号，位于说明书的第一行；正文是说明书的主体及核心部分，介绍产品的特点、使用方法、生产日期、注意事项等；落款写生产者的相关信息，方便消费者必要时联系。

必要时可配以插图或表格进行说明。

模板 1

High Grade Super Glue

Basic Info
Type：Liquid glue
Brand name：Best Glue
Model number：BG-1200
Material：Cyanoacrylate adhesive
Other name：502, super glue
Packing：Customized
Volume：3g – 30g
Packaging & Delivery
Packaging detail：3 grams/piece, 12 pieces/card, 72 cards/box

Delivery detail: 7 – 30 days

Specifications

High grade super glue contains wood, rubber, plastics, metal, leather, etc. It can bond almost all smooth surface in seconds. It requires no mixing and no heating.

Feature

Material: Cyanoacrylate adhesive

Glue percent: ≥70% or customized

Cutting strength: ≥10Mpa

Operating temperature: Around 25℃

Certification: SGS, MSDS

Bonds in: Around in 10 seconds

Specific gravity: As customized

Validity: >12 months (20℃)

Caution

1: Strong adhesion to skin, don't peel it directly if being glued, bathing within hot water for a while or wipe it off with acetone.

2: Strong smell when volatilizing. Make sure to use it under wide and air-flowing circumstance when working with it for a long time.

3: Seal the open end tightly to prevent volatilization.

4: Storage under the required condition strictly. High temperature or wetness will shorten the storage period.

5: Please keep out of reach of children.

Supplier: Yiwu Xinqi Super Glue Product Factory

Place of Production: Zhejiang China (Mainland)

Tel: 159＊＊＊＊＊581

  模板 2

Pien Tze Huang

/Medicine Name/

Proprietary name: Pien Tze Huang

Chinese pronunciation: Pianzaihuang

/**Ingredients**/ Calculus Bovis, Moschus, Radix Notoginsing, Snake's gall, etc.

/**Description**/ It's an oblate-like mass, with an oblate circle on the surface. The surface is brownish-yellow or greyish-brown, with thin serried striation and mould speckles. It is hard and uneasily broken, with brown color and a small amount of mycelia occasionally. The powder is brownish-yellow. It smells a bit fragrant and tastes bitter and a bit sweet.

/**Functions**/ Relieving internal heat and deleting toxin, cooling blood and reducing stasis, relieving swelling and stopping pain. Used for treating acute, chronic or viral hepatitis resulting from internal heat or blood stasis, ulcer and pyogenic infections, galls, injuries from falls, fractures, contusions and strains as well as all kinds of inflammations.

/**Specification**/ 3 grams per piece

/**Usage and Dosage**/ Take orally, 0.6 grams a time. For children aged under 8, take 0.15 – 0.3 grams each time. To be taken 2 – 3 times a day.

For external use, grind into powder and mix it uniformly with boiled water or vinegar, take suitable quantity and apply to the affected part for several times one day. Or adhere to the instructions of the physician.

/**Adverse Reactions**/ Not known

/**Points for Attention**/ Not to be applied by pregnant women

/**Precautions**/ Not known

/**Storage**/ Preserve in tightly closed containers, protected from moisture.

/**Packing**/ Aluminium and plastic composite-film, 3 grams × 1 piece/box

/**Period of Validity**/ Five years

/**Approval Number**/ State medical permission number Z35020243

/**Manufacturer**/ Zhangzhou Pien Tze Huang Pharmaceutical Co., Ltd.

/**Tel**/ 400-1234567

二、英文说明书编写原则

1. 说明书写作要充分考虑消费者的阅读需要，要达到"介绍产品、指导消费"这一关键目的。对于不同类型的产品，消费者有不同的阅读需求；而不同的用户，由于个性、年龄、文化程度等不同，也会有不同的需要，所以在撰写说明书时要照顾大多数消费者的需要。

2. 说明书要突出产品的特点，使消费者更好地了解产品，方便消费者使用产品。

3. 英文说明书语言要符合说明书的文本特点及英语语言习惯,语言要准确、简洁、清晰,条理要清楚。尽量避免使用难懂生僻的专业术语,防止"说而不明"。说明书不宜过长,内容要简洁明了,在排版上,要条理清楚,使消费者一目了然。

4. 说明书的内容安排要有侧重,根据产品的特点、功效、配方等突出主次,方便消费者了解产品。

5. 必要时可添加图片或表格,图文并茂,吸引消费者注意,也能更生动、更直观地介绍产品。

Unit 2

Resume

一、英文简历及其常用模板

英文简历是使用英文写的简历。英文简历并无固定不变的单一形式。一般来说,根据个人经历的不同侧重点,可以选用以下两种形式。

1. 以学历为主的简历(basic resume)

这种形式适应于应届毕业生,因为没有工作经历,所以把重点放在学业上,从最高学历往下写。在 basic resume 中,一般包括下列元素:

a. Personal Data/Information(个人资料/信息):Name(姓名)、Address(通讯地址)、Postal Code(邮政编码)、Phone Number(电话号码)、Birthdate(出生日期)、Birthplace(出生地点)、Gender(性别)、Height(身高)、Weight(体重)、Health(健康状况)、Date of Availability(可到职日期)、Number of Identification Card(身份证号码)。应届毕业生一般没有结婚,因而可省略 Marital Status(婚姻状况)和 Children(儿女情况)两项。当然,如果是毕业时已婚,则应写明。

b. Job/Career Objective(应聘职位)。

c. Education(学历):就读校系的名称、始止时间,应聘职位相关的课程与成绩,社会实践,课外活动,奖励等都应一一列出。

d. Special Skills(特别技能)。

e. Hobbies/Interests(业余爱好)。如果在学历项目的课外活动中已经注明,此项则不必重复。

 模板 1

Resume

Basic Info

Name: × × × Gender: Male
Age: 22 Date of Birth: Dec. 24th, 1994
Marital Status: Single E-mail: http://www.jianli-sky.com/
Mobile: 86-134＊＊＊＊5484 Dorm: 86-10＊＊＊＊7564

Education

Sept.,2011 – July,2015 Peking University Electronic Information Engineering Bachelor.
Major Course: C Language, Analogical Electronics, Digital Electronics, Signal and System.

Info During the School

Dec.,2014　Undertook the preliminary contest of the 1st TV Skating Competition in my college.

July,2013　Joined in Micro Freestyle Inline-Skating team as leader.

Dec.,2012　Founded the Inline-Skating Club in Peking University as the president. Now it has 200 members.

Nov.,2011　Won the first prize in Flash Designing Competition in my department.

Internship Experiences

Jan.,2013 – Feb.,2013　Baidu. com, Inc. (Beijing) Trained in Client Developing Department.

Jan.,2012 – Dec.,2012　Novots Technologies Ltd. Beijing database backup and management from VPN.

Sept.,2011 – Nov.,2011　Sikangrui Sporting Goods Beijing Campus Agent.

IT Skills

Skilled in Windows XP and Office 2007

Language Skills

Fluent oral English, CET-4 Certificate Score: 511

Self-appraisal

1. Rational, adept in planning and executing.

2. Honest, easy to communicate with; like doing things that is challenging.

3. A lot of experience in club managing and campus activities.

Career Objective

In the following three years, my target is to be a first-rank person in my field.

Other Info

Strong suit: Freestyle inline-skating.

Hobbies: Literature and all kinds of sport games.

2. 以经历为主的简历（chronological resume）

以这种形式出现的英语简历，往往侧重于工作经历，把同应聘职位有关的经历和业绩按时间顺序书写出来，把工作经历放在学历之前。工作经历和学历的时间顺序均是由近至远。毫无疑问，这种形式的英语简历适合于有工作经验的求职人员。在 chronological resume 中，通常包括以下元素：

a. Personal Data(个人资料)。具体内容与以学历为主的简历相同，不过，因为你参加工作多年，已进入结婚年龄，所以不管你是否结婚，都应注明婚姻状况和儿女情况。

b. Job/Career Objective(应聘职位)。

c. Work Experiences(工作经历)。务必写明自己在每个工作单位的职位、职责、业绩和工作起止时间。

d. Education(学历)。你已工作多年，雇主重点考虑你的工作经验是否能胜任你所应聘的职位，因此学历只是一个参考的因素，不必像以学历为主的简历那样写得详细，只需注明你就读的校系名称、始止时间和获得的学位即可。

e. Technical Qualifications and Special Skills(技术资格和特别技能)。

f. Scientific Research Achievements(科研成果)。

 模板 1

JOB OBJECTIVE

Electronics engineer in Los Angeles

BACKGROUND SUMMARY

Over eleven years of extensive computer/electronics experience. Versed in both digital and analog electronics with specific emphasis on computer hardware/software. Special expertise in system and component evaluation. Network supervisor is responsible for installing/maintaining Arcnet LAN system. Proficient in assembly and C programming languages. Excellent communication skills including writting and skeaking.

PROFESSIONAL WORK EXPERIENCES

Stevenson Data Systems, Los Angeles, CA   1995 – 2015

Components Evaluation Engineer   2014 – 2015

—Responsible for the characterization and evaluation, and approved vendors list for: Power supplies, oscillators, crystals, and programmable logic used in desktop and laptop computers. Evaluated and recommended quality components that increased product profitability. Created and developed power supply test plan used for evaluating third-party power supplies. Interacted with vendors to resolve problems associated with components qualification. Technical advisor for Purchasing. Promoted to engineer II.

Design Evaluation Engineer   2012 – 2014

—Evaluated new computer product designs, solving environmental problems on prototype computers. Conducted systems analysis on new computer products to ensure hardware, software and mechanical design integrity. Designed hardware and software for PC, ISA bus programmable load board used for environmental testing. Performed reliability lift testing on computer systems. Installed/Maintained 20 users. Novell, Arcnet LAN system. Examined system and sub-system susceptibility to electrostatic discharge in order to meet IEC-801-2 industry standards. Analyzed complete power and load of computer system and subsystem to verify power and load estimations.

Assistant Engineer   1995 – 2012

—Performed extensive hardware evaluation on prototype computers, tested prototype units for timing violation using the latest state-of-the-art test equipment, digital oscilloscopes and logic analyzers. Performed environmental, ESD and acoustic testing. Designed and built a power-up test to test prototype computers during cold boot.

EDUCATION

Bachelor of Science in Electrical Engineering

University of Southern California   1995

Associate in Engineering Electronics

University of Southern California   1991

 模板 2

× × × × ×

Languages and Literature and TESOL/TEFL

Facilitates meaningful experience for students to achieve independence and motivation during and after learning process

× × × × ×@yahoo.com/ 1 × × × × ×45678

SUMMARY

- Licensed English (Languages and Literature) Teacher
- TESOL/TEFL certified
- Professionally competent, possessing practical experience, passionate in teaching, university degree

UNIVERSITY EDUCATION

Bachelor of Secondary Education (major in English-Language and Literature, minor in Math)

× × ×　Normal University,

× × ×　City, × × ×,

The Philippines　October, 2009

TESOL/TEFL Course

Program Harvest Christian School International

(August 14, 2014 – February 25, 2015)

- Used principles, approaches, methodologies and materials in English-language teaching
- Created the lesson plan in teaching reading, phonology, writing, speaking
- Revisited grammar structure
- Discovered new trends in teaching English language to speakers of other languages

HONORS, AWARDS and ELIGIBILITIES
- Passed the License Examination for Teachers
- Recipient of University Certificate of Merit in Journalism
- Recipient of University Service and Cooperation Award
- University Scholar, from the third year to the fourth year (2007 – 2009)

EMPLOYMENT EXPERIENCE

× × ×   EDUCATION
General English Teacher
(January, 2015 – present)

- Managed class and developed critical thinking skills using age-related lesson plans for pre-school, middle school, high school, tertiary level and adults
- Collaborated in curriculum development
- Taught 1-1 IELTS/TOEFL candidates
- Used activity-based learning
- Developed self-prepared syllabus that reduced students' passivity and increased self-confidence
- Introduced activity-based learning, explained the techniques and developed sound practice

× × ×   Learning Center
Mandaluyong City, Metro Manila
Pre-school/Grade-school Reading Teacher
(December, 2010 – March, 2014)

- Taught structure of English language and reading comprehension to students aged 3 to 12
- Administered the diagnostic test and achievement test to students

- Assessed students' weaknesses and strengths
- Prepared lessons for the students
- Facilitated children's worksheets and homework
- Recorded children's performance
- Evaluated students' progress
- Checked worksheets and homework
- Used letter boards, flashcards, stories and CDs for lessons
- Communicated with parents through quarterly conferences
- Protected students' welfare during classes
- Maintained positive interactions with students, faculty and parents to ensure that the environment is conducive to learning
- Coached preschoolers for the 11th awarding ceremony reading choral

××× High school
Marasbaras, Tacloban City, Leyte
Student teacher, third-year students
(August, 2009 – October, 2009)

- Developed units using a variety of stories, materials and activities
- Constructed activities to suit students' needs and made material more engaging and meaningful
- Implemented a variety of different teaching and learning practices: cooperative and individual learning, hands-on/minds-on experiences, and informal and formal assessment
- Initiated cooperative learning projects in inclusion classes
- Introduced new materials when appropriate or necessary
- Utilized SMART board to enhance lessons

××× High School
Tacloban City, Leyte
Student teacher, first-year students
(June, 2009 – August, 2009)

- Created and implemented unit and lesson plans for four sections of English language

and literature
- Worked cooperatively with an English teacher to plan and implement lessons
- Planned learning activities for students with varied abilities
- Integrated a variety of teaching methods and instructional strategies that generated students' interest
- Tracked students' progress in class by using a combination of evaluations and student work samples

SKILLS
- Proficient in oral and written English and Filipino
- Proficient in Microsoft Word, Microsoft Powerpoint, Microsoft Excel
- Knowledgeable in basic computer hardware and software troubleshooting
- Able to work under pressure and adherent to deadlines

CHARACTER REFERENCE

× × ×
Head Instructor/Owner
× × × ×　Learning Center
Contact No.

× × ×
Supervisor
× × × ×　Learning Center
Contact No.

二、英文简历编写原则

英文简历和一般中文简历的表现方式稍有不同。一份能够积极展现个人特色、优点以及潜力的英文履历是比较容易得到面试者青睐的。那么,英文简历的书写有哪些基本原则呢?

1. 勇于表现个人风格,不拘泥于形式

英文简历没有所谓的固定形式,你必须衡量自身以及职务需求,采用最能凸显优势的内容呈现方式,格式要自行设计。以所附的模板为例,有时候你不一定要写出 Professional Qualities(专业技能)这项。

2. 内容以条例编排为最高原则

人事主管每天要看的履历很多,停留在一份履历的时间不超过 20 秒,因此建议将内容以条例方式呈现,让人事主管能在短时间内抓住这份履历的重点。

3. 尽量控制在两张纸以内

一份厚厚的简历对忙碌的人事主管来说会比较头疼。因此应多费一点心思来设计你的版面,尽量控制在两张纸以内。

4. 搭配求职信(coverletter)

求职信兼任自我推荐的作用,是英文简历不可或缺的部分。另外,在撰写简历以及求职信时,可以参考你个人工作经历的长短以及是否有职业上的转型等来做一些重点调整。

5. 英文简历并不需要附上照片

除非应聘的公司有所要求,否则一般不需要贴上照片。

Unit 3

Notice

一、英文通知及其常用模板

通知主要是机关团体用来传达事务或布置工作用的,通常用于上级对下级或组织对成员布置工作、传达事情或召集会议等。通知的一般形式主要有以下三种。

1. 口头通知(announcement)

口头通知是一方向另一方口头传达的通知,具有以下特点:

① 用词口语化,表达言简意赅,简洁明了。

② 无须写通知时间和发通知的单位。

③ 开头可有称呼语,具体因通知对象而异。常用的称呼语有"Ladies and gentlemen""Boys and girls""Teachers and fellow students",也有的不用开头语,直接正文。

④ 开头语和结束语常有一些惯用表达,如开头语:"Attention, please!""Listen, please!""May I have your attention, please?""I have good news for you all."结束语:"That's all. Thank you.""Please attend/come to it on time.""Please be there on time.""Do come on time.""Any questions?""Does everyone understand?"

⑤ 句子多用简单句和祈使句,时态多用将来时,语态多用被动。

模板 1

Boys and girls,

    May I take your attention, please? There will be a lecture at half past three on Friday afternoon. It's about "Internet + English Study". And it will be given by Mr. Joseph, who is a famous teacher from the English Department. There's sure to have something instructive and interesting. We can get more information from it, I think. And it will improve our English studies to a new stage. Anyone who wants to attend it can come to Room 208. Take notes and have a discussion after it.

    Please be there on time. That's all. Thank you.

 模板 2

Ladies and gentlemen

    May I have your attention, please? I have an announcement to make. This afternoon we will visit the Windows of the World. All the tourists should gather at the gate of our hotel at 2:30 p.m., on Friday, May 6th, 2016. We will start out by bus. All of us will wear the red caps and take water and snacks by ourselves. After entering it, we can visit every place freely and take photos. I think it will be very interesting. We will get back at 6:00 p.m. by bus. The bus will stop at the exit. Don't be late. That's all. Thank you.

2. 书面通知（notice）

书面通知是以书面的形式表达通知内容，通常以布告、张贴的形式出现在显眼的位置，书面通知的写作格式和特点如下：

① 用语书面化，措辞较严谨，句子结构相对复杂。

② 开头有标题，通常为 Notice，居中，为了醒目，标题的每个字母可大写。

③ 标题之下是正文，正文包括事件或活动的内容、通知对象、具体的时间、地点以及注意事项或要求。

④ 落款部分是出通知的单位和出通知的时间。单位一般置于正文的右下角，时间位

于标题左上角。

⑤ 时态以一般将来时为主,常用第三人称,语态多用被动。

  模板 3

NOTICE

Jan. 5th, 2016

  A meeting is going to be held in Room 305 of Teaching Building 1 at 7:30 p.m. on Jan. 10th. Issues to be discussed at the meeting include the safety of the dormitories, proper use of electricity, what to do in case of fire, and prevention of swindle and so on. A member of each dormitory is required to be presented. All the presented should take notebooks with them and arrive on time. They should take notes carefully and after the meeting they are to inform their roommates of what is discussed and what measures will be taken.

The Dormitory Committee

  模板 4

NOTICE

Jan. 6th, 2016

  All the students of the Department of Computer and Information are required to attend the lecture in the auditorium at 3:00 p.m. on Tuesday, Jan. 9th. The lecture will be given by Professor Lee on how to make flash. And all the students are expected to be present on time.

The Students' Union of the Department of Computer and Information

3. 海报式通知(poster notice)

  海报式通知是日常生活中常见的一种通告形式,多用于电影、戏曲、文艺演出、讲座、比赛等社会活动。海报式通知的特点如下:

  ① 用语简明扼要,形式新颖美观。

② 内容包括活动性质、主办单位、活动时间及地点。
③ 格式通常包括标题、正文、落款。

 模板 5

The Graduation Party

Jun. 13th, 2016

  Graduate students of the Economic Management Department will bring wonderful and joyful programs of entertainment to the teachers and fellow students to let them enjoy the happiness of graduation at 7:30 p.m. on Saturday (Jun. 16th) in the auditorium.

  Admission free.

The Students' Union of the Economic Management Department

 模板 6

Academic Lecture

By American-Chinese Scholar

March 7th, 2016

Theme: International Business Etiquette

Lecturer: Professor Mike Chen

Time: 9:00 a.m., Friday, March 11th

Place: Lecture Room 307, Teaching Building 2

Sponsor: All the students of the English Department

The Department Office

模板 7

The Film

Apr. 7th, 2016
At this Friday
Title: He Is a Dragon
Time: 6:00 p.m., Friday, Apr. 13th
Place: The School Auditorium
Sponsor: The Film Group
Free Admission

The Film Club

二、英文通知撰写原则

英文通知无论是哪一种形式,均要着重掌握其撰写格式和在正文中时态的运用。其主体内容均包括通知对象、事由、时间、地点、主办机构等。英文通知表达上言简意赅,简洁明了,多用将来时和被动语态。但是不同形式的通知又有不同的撰写原则。

1. 口头通知开头有一些常用称呼语,结尾有结束语。发通知的时间和发通知的单位无须注明。用语尽量口语化,常用简单句和祈使句。

2. 书面通知的标题要居中,并且为了引人注意,每个字母常用大写,书面通知的用语要书面化,避免使用模糊、不规范的语言,书面通知可以使用一些长句,人称常用第三人称。正文结束后的右下方要署发通知的单位。

3. 海报式通知的标题往往切中主题,直接揭示通知的内容,并且形式上追求新颖美观,内容多以条例形式进行编排。

4. 英文书面通知出具通知的时间常置于标题左上方,与汉语的出具通知的时间位于落款之下不同。

5. 无论何种通知,均要措辞得当,发布及时。

Unit 4
Type of Letters

A. Cover Letter

一、求职信及其常用模板

求职信是求职者写给招聘单位的信函。求职信属于简历的附信,放在简历的前面或者后面。求职信格式并不固定,一般包含 3 到 5 个简短的段落,并通常包含以下几个要素:

a. 写信表明求职意愿。
b. 自我介绍,如:个人情况、个人能力、工作经历、工作技能和专长等。
c. 请求面试机会。
d. 表达感谢。
e. 附件,如:简历、毕业证书、资格证书、推荐信等。

 模板 1

Dear Sir or Madam,
　　I'm very excited and delighted over the good news that you are recruiting a sales manager. I once worked in the Golden Star Automobile Company Beijing Office and was in charge of the sale of different vehicles, such as sedans, SUVs, mini vans, etc. As a district sales manager, I have 3 years of working experience and I'm quite confident that my abilities can meet your requirements.

Enclosed is my resume. I hope you will consider my application. Thank you for your time.

Look forward to hearing from you soon!

Sincerely yours,
Li Ming

 模板 2

Dear Sir or Madam,

　　I'm writing to apply for the position of secretary advertised in the newspaper of March 20th, 2016.

　　I'm twenty-two years old and a graduate of Lushan College of Guangxi University of Science and Technology. From the enclosed resume, I hope you can see that I am well-qualified for the job. With one year of part-time secretarial experience, I am skilled at dealing with routine office work, and have rich experience in word-processing of both Chinese and English.

　　I've long been interested in working for your company, and I believe that, by joining a company as famous and well-respected as your own, I can fully realize my potential. I am confident that my ability and experience will fully qualify me for the position.

　　I would appreciate it if you can grant me an interview. You can reach me at 53678921.

　　I'm looking forward to your reply.

Sincerely yours,
Li Ming

二、求职信的撰写原则

　　在找工作的过程中，一封漂亮的求职信就如同一位出色的"使者"，可以让人印象深刻，增加获得面试的机会，因此如何设计求职信是关键。一般而言，求职信有以下几个撰写原则：

　　1. 求职信属于非正式的信函，它必须能够在双方之间建立融洽的气氛。因此，热情洋溢和令人振奋的语言会更好地感染对方。同时一定要注意用词简洁准确，态度不卑不六。传达的信息可信度高,而在介绍自身经历和优点时,也应该把握尺度。

2. 在开头部分,要简单说明你从何处看到招聘广告或得到招聘信息、你对哪个职位比较感兴趣,这可明确你的来信目的。

3. 求职信中必须向招聘者即你未来的雇主介绍你的长处。如果有必要还要说明自己换工作的理由。

4. 在结尾部分,请求面试机会,这也是写求职信的目的所在。因此,结尾提出自己的希望,请求招聘单位安排面试,并告知对方你的联系方式。同时还要表达感谢,以留下好印象。

5. 注意附件。随信附上个人简历和相关证件等,特别是招聘单位需要的材料须在信中注明。

6. 信件简短扼要,篇幅 3 到 5 段为宜。在信末必须手写签名。

B. The Letter of Invitation

一、邀请信及其常用模板

邀请信是在社交场合中邀请对方参加活动或出席会议时写的信件。邀请信分为两种:一种属于个人信函,例如,邀请某人参加宴会、出席典礼、共进晚餐等;另一种则属于商务信函,一般邀请参加会议、学术活动等。邀请信通常包含以下几个部分:

a. 邀请对方参加活动的内容以及举行此项活动的目的。
b. 提供细节,如:时间、地点等。
c. 如有必要,请对方回复邀请信。

模板 1

> Dear Mr. Smith,
>
>   To celebrate the 10th anniversary of ABC Company, we are planning to hold a dinner party at the Hilton Hotel in Guangzhou from 7:30 p.m. to 11:00 p.m. on Friday, July 20th.
>
>   We take pleasure in inviting you to attend our special party.
>
>   We should be very delighted if you could honor us with your presence.
>
> Sincerely yours,
Li Ming

模板 2

> Dear Sir or Madam,
> 　　We would like to invite you to an exclusive presentation of our new PAOJUN. The presentation will take place at the Renaissance Hotel in Liuzhou, at 10:00 a.m. on October 10th. We hope you and your colleagues will be able to attend.
> 　　ABC Automobile Company is a leading producer of high quality. As you well know, recent technological advances have been made increasingly affordable to the public. Our new models offer superb quality and sophistication with economy, and their new features give them distinct advantages over similar products from other manufacturers.
> 　　Please respond on or before September 20th, 2015. We look forward to hearing from you soon.
> 　　　　　　　　　　　　　　　　　　　　　　　　　　　Sincerely yours,
> 　　　　　　　　　　　　　　　　　　　　　　　　　　　Li Ming

二、邀请信的撰写原则

邀请信通常可以分为两种：普通邀请信和正式邀请信。第一种邀请信邀请的对象一般是朋友、熟人，所以内容和格式上的要求不高，篇幅也相对较短，只需要写清楚活动内容、时间、地点等即可。第二种邀请信一般由会议或学术活动的组委会的某一负责人写，以组委会的名义发出去，通常被邀请的人都是较有威望的人士。因此，在措辞方面要相对正式。信件中除了活动名称、时间、地点外，要表明如果被邀请者能够接受邀请，会给会议或者学术活动带来哪些帮助，最好能吸引对方。同时不要忘记表达希望对方参加的诚意，最后还要请收信人对发出的邀请做出反馈。

C. The Letter of Recommendation

一、推荐信及其常用模板

推荐信是一个人为推荐另一个人去接受某个职位或参与某项工作而写的信件。英文推荐信会因推荐人的不同而在内容的侧重点上有所不同。但是通常包含以下几个部分：

  a. 推荐者姓名、职位、公司名称、地址等。

  b. 简单介绍自己的背景、自己与被推荐人的关系、推荐他/她的目的。

  c. 陈述被推荐人的工作经历或个人特点，如：在工作、学习、为人、性格等方面的优点。重点突出他/她的技术、完成的任务、对公司或社会的贡献等。

  d. 结尾部分向收件人表示感谢和期待。

模板 1

Dear Mr. Smith,

  It's my honor to recommend my student Mr. Li Ming as an ideal candidate for the position.

  Mr. Li graduated in machinery from Sun Yat-Sen University two years ago, and he has one and a half years of work experience of being an engineer. Moreover, he is an excellent employee with a high sense of responsibility, good team work spirit and positive working attitude. I believe he would be a valuable asset to your company.

  Therefore, I don't hesitate to recommend him as the right person for the position. Should you have any further inquiries, please feel free to contact me at 5643-9812.

Sincerely,
Wang Dong
Professor, Dean
College of Engineering, Sun Yat-Sen University

模板 2

To Whom It May Concern,

  I'm writing to recommend one of my assistants Li Jing for this position. I've known her for two years as her team leader. She is a very intelligent young woman with a bright personality, good team spirit. What's more, she is always working hard and eager to improve herself.

续表

All in all, it is both my pleasure and honor to write this recommendation letter for Ms. Li. I'm sure you will make a wise decision in hiring her. Please contact me at 2457-5689 if you need any further information.

Sincerely yours,
John Smith
General Manager
ABC China
Tel：+86 10 2457-5689
E-mail：jsmith@abc.com
Address：Rm. 1801, International Finance Square
567 Jianguomenwai Avenue, Beijing, 100020

二、推荐信的撰写原则

推荐信是申请新职位或出国留学申请中的必备材料。一封好的推荐信可以让你事半功倍，起到关键作用。一般而言，写推荐信时要注意以下几个原则：

1. 选择与被推荐人有过密切关系，熟悉其领导能力、组织能力或学术水平的人写推荐信。推荐人必须客观公正、实事求是地评价，切忌不切实际地浮夸。

2. 选择真正欣赏被推荐人的人，只有这样的推荐人才愿意花时间和精力写好一封推荐信。

3. 选择能够说明被推荐人的良好品质和性格的人。他/她能态度诚恳，言之有理、言之有据地陈述被推荐人在管理、为人处事等方面的能力，最重要的是能用具体的事例进行举例说明。

Unit 5
Abstract

一、摘要的概念

科技文章的摘要是整个文章的浓缩,放在文章标题和正文之间,是对文章的主要内容准确而简明地表述,读者在最短时间内通过阅读摘要来了解文章的主旨和主要信息,所以摘要是科技文献检索的重要途径。

二、摘要的篇幅和结构

科技文章摘要的长度,根据文章长度,一般为论文字数的3%—5%。如果论文为4000—5000字/词,该摘要大概120—250字/词。也可以根据实际情况,进行变通,如果论文研究内容很前沿,其摘要往往也趋于详尽。

"摘要"一般包括五部分:(1)文章的研究背景,(2)研究目的、对象和研究问题,(3)研究方法,(4)研究结果或发现,(5)总结或者启示。背景是针对文章所关注领域的文献综述,即前人研究成果和进一步研究的价值。第二部分是指文章所研究的范围、目的和意义。方法指的是在研究过程中具体采用的研究手段。结果指的是研究所取得的数据和效果。最后是对研究结果的分析和评价。其顺序可以根据文章本身的性质,进行适当的调整。一般情况下都会将文章的核心部分详细写,或是内容上的独特性和定量或者定性的关键信息,或是方法的创新,或是文章的发现,或是详细的结论等。有的摘要只有一段,也有的摘要有几段。不管如何,最主要的是要将文章最重要的内容清楚地表达出来。例如:

Abstract

(1) Although participation in volunteering and motivation to volunteer (MTV) has received substantial attention on the national level, particularly in the U. S., few studies have compared and explained these issues across cultural and political contexts. (2) This study compares how two theoretical perspectives, social origins theory and signaling theory, and explains variations in MTV across different

countries. (3) The study analyzes responses from a sample of 5,794 students from six countries representing distinct institutional context. (4) The findings provide strong support for signaling theory but less so for social origins theory. (5) The article concludes that volunteering is a personal decision and thus is influenced more at the individual level but is also impacted to some degree by macro-level societal forces.

Source: Hustinx, L. et al. (2010). Social and cultural origins of motivation to volunteer: A comparison of university students in six countries. *International Sociology*, 25 (3).

这则摘要一共5句话,简单扼要地介绍了论文的研究背景、研究目的、研究问题、研究方法、研究结果和结论。第一句话是研究背景和目的。目前论文所研究领域,即志愿者志愿活动和动机(MTV)的研究局限在国家层面,很少有论文从不同文化或者政治背景进行研究。这也就是本论文的研究出发点和意义。第二句话是论文的研究目的和研究问题,即比较社会根源理论(social origins theory)和信号理论(signaling theory)是怎样解释不同国家MTV以及存在的差异。第三句话是研究方法和研究范围,即对来自6个不同国家的5794名志愿者的样本分析(a sample of 5,794 students from six countries)。第四句话是论文的研究结果,即信号理论比社会根源理论更能够为论文提供支撑。第五句话则是论文的总结:志愿者行为更多的是个人意愿,虽然宏观的社会环境有一点影响。

三、摘要的写作特点

1. 词汇特点

科技文章以专业人员为阅读群体,属于正式文体,用词正规,既无方言、俗语、俚语等的口语色彩,又无情感上的好恶和褒贬,给人一种平稳、庄重的感觉。普通词通常词义明确,通俗易懂,但又因为其专业性,往往也有专业化程度高的术语和非言语符号。例如:

Practice guidelines do not recommend use of an implantable cardioverter-defibrillator (ICD) for primary prevention in patients recovering from a myocardial infarction or coronary artery bypass graft surgery and those with severe heart failure symptoms or a recent diagnosis of heart failure.

这是一篇题为"Non-evidence-Based ICD Implantations in the United States"的医学科技论文摘要的第一段。出现了诸如 myocardial infarction(心肌梗塞)、coronary artery bypass graft surgery(冠状动脉旁路移植手术)等医学专业用词,和缩写词 ICD(埋藏式复律除颤器)。其他词汇是普通词汇,但是要理解摘要内容本身,读者必须对专业词汇非常熟悉。

2. 基本原则

科技文章摘要的语言必须坚持准确、简洁和清楚的原则。准确指的是摘要紧扣文章主题;简洁指的是用最少的篇幅表达最完整的内容;清楚指的是用规范的语言明确阐述论文的研究对象、方法、结果和结论,不带任何感情色彩和不确定的意义。例如:

Abstract

(1) The aim of this paper is to seek an answer to a specific question: How to make city logistics sustainable? (2) This question in principle has no specific answer. (3) By contrast, it could be answered in many and varied ways. (4) Behind the search for some of these answers lies the development of a roadmap which this work aims to present. (5) The research lines, the theoretical framework and methodology of the roadmap will be explained. (6) Although the current status of the roadmap, its duration and timing still need to be completed, the main facts, as well as the results obtained to date and the expected results are here presented.

Source: Rafael Grosso-delaVega et al. (2015). Quantitative assessment of sustainable city logistics. *International Journal of Production Management and Engineering*, 3(2):97–101.

摘要第一句话就简明扼要地说明了论文所研究的问题:如何使城市物流可持续发展?第四句话清楚写明该论文给出的答案:路线图及其发展(Behind the search for some of these answers lies the development of a roadmap which this work aims to present)。进而第五句话进一步说明该论文会详细解释路线图的研究过程、理论框架和方法论。很明显,从这三句话,我们就能清晰得知该论文的主要内容和主要任务。而第二、三句是学术论文语言精准性的表现,也可以说是本论文的研究背景。对于论文研究问题,论文作者都需要做一定的前期研究和文献综述,总结国内外对此的研究成果和研究现状,但是作者的前期研究并不一定就能完全包含实际上所有的研究成果,因此这两句话是必需的,也符合论文摘要的准确性原则。

3. 常用时态和语态

科技文章英语摘要在写作上常用一般现在时。其他时态,根据实际,比如一般过去式、一般将来时和现在完成时也出现在科技论文的摘要中。语态上主动语态和被动语态都常用。

一般现在时结合主动语态用得最多。一般现在时用于说明研究目的、叙述研究内容、描述结果、得出结论、提出建议或讨论等。涉及公认事实、自然规律、永恒真理等。谓语动词在多数情况下采用主动语态，以此来表明文章作者的研究目的和意图。例如：

a. This paper discusses the achievements in computer science and its further development in the next 10 years.

b. Finally, this paper gives an overall conclusion on current development of relief development forecasting method.

现在完成时一般多见于作者所做的文献综述中。例如：
Although participation in volunteering and motivation to volunteer (MTV) have received substantial attention on the national level, particularly in the U. S., few studies have compared and explained these issues across cultural and political contexts.

一般过去时用于叙述过去某一时刻的发现、某一研究过程（实验、观察、调查、医疗等过程），所描述的研究过程也明显带有过去时间的痕迹。一般将来时用于描述论文的研究过程和即将采用的研究方法等。通常这两种时态都与被动语态连用。被动语态强调事实的经过，强调动作承受者，强调的事物作主语，因此被动语态能突出科技文章的科学性、严谨性、准确性。例如：

a. The structure of dislocation core in gap was investigated by weak-beam electro microscope.

b. The research lines, the theoretical framework and methodology of the roadmap will be explained.

c. In this paper, relief will be categorized from point view of government and academia, to explain the relationship between relief categorization and demand forecasting.

d. In this case, a greater accuracy in measuring distance might be obtained.

总的来说，科技论文英文摘要在其发展和演变的过程中，逐渐形成有别于其他文体的特点。同一篇摘要，有研究的背景、目的、范围、方法、手段、步骤、结果以及研究得出的主要结论等，涉及不同的时空过程，因而几种时态交替出现，也体现了科技论文英语摘要的时态特征。现将各项对应的时态列示如下：(1)研究的背景、目的、范围——常用现在完成时、一般现在时；(2)研究的方法、手段、步骤——常用一般过去时、一般现在时或现在

完成时;(3)研究的结果——常用一般过去时、一般将来时;(4)研究得出的主要结论——常用现在时。例如:

Abstract

The article discusses the logistics of the Republic of Guinea and its impacts on the environment. The main problems are the emissions of greenhouse gases and other air pollutants, noise, and the tightness of surfaces due to building of infrastructure in the transport sector. Optimization of the supply chain is most often focused on finding the optimization, of flow of costs, time, quality criteria and services. For the use of multi-criteria combinatorial optimization uses several methods to support the optimization, such as the method of multi-criteria decision-making or optimization methods.

Following the requirements of sustainable development and green marketing, solutions is offered to reduce the pollution created by the logistics infrastructure. But the solutions do not take into account some of the aspects and critical issues that remain unresolved. As a result, we can summarize various elements describing the changes of the environment, such as pressure on the environment, the impact on the population, economy, ecosystems and the response of the society.

Source: Aly Hawa CAMARA et al. (2015). The influence of logistics on the environment in Republic of Guinea. *Sibiu Alma Mater University Journals.* 8(1).

4. 英文摘要常用句式

1) This paper deals with ...

2) This article focuses on the topics of ...

3) This essay presents knowledge that ...

4) This thesis discusses ...

5) This paper provides an overview of ...

6) This paper elaborates on ...

7) This article gives an overview of ...

8) This paper provides a method of ...

9) The writer of this paper discusses ...

10) This paper strongly emphasizes ...

11) This paper presents up to date information on ...

12) This article not only describes ... but also suggests ...

13) This paper includes discussions concerning …

14) This article compares … and summarizes key findings.

15) This paper introduces an applicable procedure to analyze …

16) This paper offers the latest information regarding …

17) This paper is devoted to examining the role of …

18) This paper addresses important topics including …

19) This paper reports the latest information on …

20) The objective of this paper is to explore …

21) The purpose of this article is to review/prove/show/present/develop/generalize/investigate …

Unit 6

Reference

一、参考文献的类型及规范

参考文献是在学术研究过程中,对某一著作或论文的参考或借鉴。按照 GB/T 7714—2005《文后参考文献著录规则》的定义,文后参考文献是指"为撰写或编辑论文和著作而引用的有关文献信息资源"。

参考文献的顺序一般是:英文资料在前,中文资料在后。按照作者姓名首字母的先后顺序排列。

参考文献的参考准则主要有 American Psychological Association(APA)和 Modern Language Association(MLA)两种格式,APA 格式强调出版物的年代(Time of the Publication Year),而不大注重原文作者的姓名。引文时常将出版年代置于作者缩写的名(the Initial of Author's First Name)之前。中国的外语类期刊(以语言学刊物为主)及自然科学类的学术刊物常使用 APA 格式。MLA 格式是美国现代语言协会制定的论文指导格式,在书写英语论文时一般使用 MLA 格式,且引用文章的作者及参考文章的页码直接标注在正文内容中,如:(Murray,39)。下面将介绍 MLA 格式以及 APA 格式的书写。

二、MLA 引用格式

1. 书籍格式

(1) 当书籍只有一个作者时(注:当书籍没有作者时,参考文献中不需要标注作者名)

作者名. *书籍名*. 出版地:出版商, 出版日期.

例如:Gell-Mann, Murray. *The Quark and the Jaguar: Adventures in the Simple and the Complex*. New York:Freeman, 1994.

(2) 当书籍有两个或三个作者时

所有作者名. *书籍名*. 出版地:出版商, 出版日期.

例如：Laplanche, Jean & Jean-Bertrand Pontalis. *Vocabulaire de la Psychanalyse.* Paris：PUF, 1973.

（3）当书籍有三个以上作者时

所有作者名（或第一作者名,et al）. *书籍名*. 出版地：出版商, 出版日期.

例如：Gilman, Sander, et al. *Hysteria beyond Freud.* Berkeley：University of California Press, 1993.

（4）当书籍属于网络书籍时

作者名. *书籍名*. 出版时间. 组织机构. 刊登时间. <阅读网址>.

例如：Latner, Richard B. *Crisis at Fort Sumter.* 1996. Tulane University. Feb. 14, 1998. <http://www.tulane.edu/~latner/CrisisMain.html>.

（5）由相同的一个或几个作者写的两本或以上的书籍

作者名. *书籍名*. 出版地：出版商, 出版日期.

… *书籍名*. 出版地：出版商, 出版日期.

例如：Frye, Northrop. *Anatomy of Criticism: Four Essays.* Princeton：Princeton University Press, 1957.

… *The Double Vision: Language and Meaning in Religion.* Toronto：University of Toronto Press, 1991.

（6）当作者是一个组织或团体时

组织名. *书籍名*. 出版地：出版商, 出版日期.

例如：Public Agenda Foundation. *The Health Care Crisis: Containing Costs, Expanding Coverage.* New York：McGraw-Hill, 1992.

（7）一本书籍有多个出版商时,须列出各个出版商

作者名. *书籍名*. 出版地：出版商, 出版日期；出版地：出版商, 出版日期.

例如：Wells, H. G. *The Time Machine.* London：Dent, 1895；Rutland：Tuttle, 1992.

（8）翻译图书须注明翻译者；当书有好几个版本时,须注明是第几版本；有编者名时,须注明编者名

例如：Hildegard of Bingen. *Selected Writings.* Trans. Mark Atherton. New York：Penguin, 2001.

Chaucer, Geoffrey. *The Works of Geoffrey Chaucer*（2nd ed.）. Ed. F. N. Robinson. Boston：Houghton, 1957.

2. 文章格式

（1）期刊文章

作者. "文章名". *期刊名*. 卷号（出版日期）：页码.

例如：Mason, Richard. "How Things Happen? Divine-Natural Law in Spinoza". *Studia Leibnitiana.* 28（1996）：17 – 36.

（2）在线期刊文章

作者．"文章名"．*期刊名*．卷号．期号（出版日期）：页码．网络．检索时间．

例如：Wheelis, Mark. "Frontiers in Bio-science 3". *Gene Therapy Approach*. 8. 3 (1998): 57-75. Web. Feb. 8, 1998.

（3）报纸文章

作者．"文章名"．*报纸名*．出版日期，版本：报纸版数．

例如：Jeromack, Paul. "This Once, a David of the Art World Does Goliath a Favor". *New York Times*. July 13, 2002, New England ed.: A13+.

三、APA 格式

1. 期刊格式

（1）中文期刊格式

作者（出版日期）．文章名．期刊名，期别，页码．

例如：仲伟合（2010）．口译研究的"名"与"实"．中国翻译，4, 7—8．

（2）英文期刊格式

第一作者 & 第二作者（出版日期）．文章名．期刊名，卷号（期号），页码．

例如：Powers, J. M. & Cookson, P. W. Jr. (1999). The politics of school choice research. *Educational Policy*, 13(1), 104-122.

2. 书籍格式

（1）中文书籍格式

作者（出版日期）．书名．出版地：出版商．

例如：陈家瑞（2009）．汽车构造（第三版）．北京：机械工业出版社．

（2）英文书籍格式

作者（出版日期）．*书名*（第几版）．出版地：出版商．

例如：Rosenthal, R. (1987). *Meta-analytic Procedures for Social Research* (2nd ed.). Newbury Park, CA: Sage.

Appendix

1. 常见院系名称双语对照

大学	University
学院	College/School/Academy/Institute/University
研究生院	Graduate School
工学院	College of Engineering
理学院	College of Science
文学院	College of Liberal Arts
教育学院	School of Education
职业技术学院	Vocational and Technical College
戏剧学院	School of Drama
音乐学院	School of Music
美术学院	College of Fine Arts/Academy of Art
外贸学院	College of Foreign Trade
体育学院	Institute of Physical Education/Sport University/Sport Institute
电影学院	College of Film/Film Academy
舞蹈学院	Dance Academy
商学院	College of Business
林学院	Forestry Institute
农学院	College of Agriculture
铁道学院	Railway Institute
外交学院	Institute of Diplomacy/Foreign Affairs University
艺术学院	School of Arts/Arts University
国际关系学院	University of International Relations
现代远程教育学院	School of Modern Distance Education
石油大学	University of Petroleum

地质大学	Geological University
航空航天大学	University of Aeronautics and Astronautics
国防大学	National Defense University
医科大学	University of Medical Sciences
海洋大学	Ocean University
军医大学	Military Medical University
政法大学	University of Political Science and Law
师范大学	Normal University
民族大学	Nationalities University
科技大学	University of Science and Technology
外国语大学	International Studies University
财经大学	University of Finance and Economics
传媒大学	University of Media and Communication
广播电视大学	Radio and Television University
工业大学	University of Technology
机械工程系	Mechanical Engineering
汽车工程系	Automotive Engineering
土木工程系	Civil Engineering
电气与计算机工程系	Electrical and Computer Engineering
经济管理系	Economics and Management
食品与化学工程系	Food and Chemical Engineering
艺术与设计系	Art and Design
外语系	Foreign Language and Literature Department
体育系	Department of Physical Education
数学科学系	Mathematical Science Department
护理学系	Nursing Science Department
文化传媒系	Culture and Media Department
音乐表演系	Music Performance Department

2. 常见大学专业学科双语对照

哲学	Philosophy
逻辑学	Logic
伦理学	Ethics

美学	Aesthetics
宗教学	Science of Religion
经济学	Economics
金融学	Finance
统计学	Statistics
法学	Law
政治学	Political Science
外交学	Diplomacy
社会学	Sociology
人口学	Demography
民族学	Ethnology
民俗学	Folklore
教育学	Education
课程与教学论	Curriculum and Teaching Methodology
高等教育学	Higher Education
心理学	Psychology
体育学	Physical Education
文学	Literature
外国语言文学	Foreign Language and Literature
新闻传播学	Journalism and Communication
音乐学	Music
史学	History
理学	Natural Science
数学	Mathematics
概率论与数理统计	Probability and Mathematical Statistics
物理学	Physics
化学	Chemistry
天文学	Astronomy
天体物理	Astrophysics
地理学	Geography
大气科学	Atmospheric Sciences
气象学	Meteorology
海洋科学	Marine Sciences
地质学	Geology
生物学	Biology

生态学	Ecology
工学	Engineering
力学	Mechanics
机械工程	Mechanical Engineering
车辆工程	Vehicle Engineering
光学工程	Optical Engineering
材料科学与工程	Materials Science and Engineering
材料加工工程	Materials Processing Engineering
冶金工程	Metallurgical Engineering
冶金物理化学	Physical Chemistry of Metallurgy
热能工程	Thermal Power Engineering
电气工程	Electrical Engineering
信息与通信工程	Information and Communication Engineering

3. 常见专业技术职称名称双语对照

教授	professor
副教授	associate professor
讲师	lecturer
助教	assistant
高级教师	senior teacher
一级教师	first-grade teacher
二级教师	second-grade teacher
三级教师	third-grade teacher
主任医师	professor of medicine
副主任医师	associate professor of medicine
主治医师	consultant
医师	doctor
药师	pharmacist
护士	nurse
护士长	head nurse
高级工程师	senior engineer
工程师	engineer
助理工程师	assistant engineer

技术员	technician
高级经济师	senior economist
经济师	economist
助理经济师	assistant economist
经济员	economic clerk
高级编辑	senior editor
主任编辑	associate senior editor
编辑	editor
助理编辑	assistant editor
播音指导	director of announcing
主任播音员	chief announcer
一级播音员	first-grade announcer
二级播音员	second-grade announcer
三级播音员	third-grade announcer
研究员	professor
副研究员	associate research fellow
助理研究员	assistant researeh fellow
研究实习员	research assistant
国家级教练	national coach
高级教练	senior coach
一级教练	first-grade coach
二级教练	second-grade coach
三级教练	third-grade coach
译审	senior translator
副译审	associate senior translator
翻译	translator
助理翻译	assistant translator
工艺美术师	industrial artist
农艺师	agronomist
导演	director
演员	actor/actress
记者	reporter
公证员	notary public
高级会计师	senior accountant
会计师	accountant

助理会计师	assistant accountant
会计员	junior accountant

4. 常见公司企业各部门名称双语对照

总公司	Head Office
分公司	Branch Office
营业部	Business Office
人力资源部	Human Resources Department
总务部	General Affairs Department
财务部	General Accounting Department
销售部	Sales Department
国际部	International Department
出口部	Export Department
进口部	Import Department
公共关系	Public Relations Department
广告部	Advertising Department
企划部	Planning Department
产品开发部	Product Development Department
研发部	Research and Development Department
秘书室	Secretarial Room

参考答案及解析

阅读基础篇

Unit 1

Text A

Ⅰ.

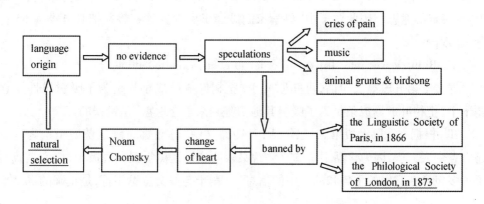

Ⅱ.

1. d 2. e 3. a 4. c 5. b 6. i 7. g 8. j 9. f 10. h

Ⅲ.

1. D. 根据原文第一段段意:声音无法像化石一样传承,所以使得语言起源的研究更加困难。题目问的是什么使得对语言起源的研究更加困难,因此选择 D。

2. D. 根据原文第四段段意:这些推测认为语言始于痛苦的喊叫,后来才慢慢形成清晰的单词。还有人认为语言起源于音乐,或者源于人们对兽类或鸟类声音的模仿。题目 A、B、C 选项分别指鸟叫、音乐、痛苦的喊叫,皆是文中所提,因此选择 D。

3. B. 根据原文第四段段意:1866 年,巴黎语言学协会终于对这些天马行空的揣测忍无可忍,禁止任何有关语言起源的交流。而英国的语言学家们在这件事情上也持相同的观点,因此选择 B。

4. C. 根据原文第五段段意:麻省理工的语言学家诺姆·乔姆斯基认为儿童之所以可以轻松地习得语言,一定有其生物学基础,因此选择 C。

5. B. 根据原文第五段段意：在这一观点的基础上，乔姆斯基的一些同事提出了他们的主张——语言的进化就像眼睛和翅膀一样，也是自然选择的结果，因此选择 B。

Text B

Ⅰ.

1. F. Previous studies have only revealed chimps could communicate with posture, but can't show what each posture means.

根据文章第一段第三句话，可知原文表达的是"虽然先前的研究已经揭示，黑猩猩会用姿势进行交流，但一直没有人详细研究它们的每一种姿势是什么意思"，因此题干中"还阐释了每一种姿势的含义"的信息是错误的。

2. T. 根据文章第一段第二句话中"黑猩猩是与人类相近的动物"可知科学家们也正因为如此才选择黑猩猩进行长期研究。

3. F. Scientists discovered that wild chimps communicate 19 specific messages to one another with a lexicon of 66 gestures.

根据文章第三段第一句话，可知"他们发现野生黑猩猩使用了 66 种姿势语言，可以表达 19 种特定的意思"，因此题干中"科学家们破译了黑猩猩的姿势并把其分类为 66 种表达"是错误的。

4. F. Biting leaves into strips is in order to elicit sexual attention.

根据文章第五段第二句话，可知原文中"把树叶撕咬成小片是为了吸引异性注意"，而题干中"把树叶成撕成条是为了吸引其他黑猩猩来争夺地盘"是错误的。

5. T. 根据文章第七段第二、三句话，可知原文中"苏珊娜·舒尔茨博十认为这个研究还有点令人失望，因为含糊不清的手势含义表明也许是黑猩猩交流极少，也许是我们遗漏了很多包含在它们的手势和动作中的信息"。题干与原文意思相符，是正确的。

Ⅱ.

1. They have revealed that chimps could communicate with gestures, and apes and monkeys can understand complex information from another animal's call.

2. It is to find out each gesture meaning and provide valuable reference to trace the origin of human languages.

3. They discovered that wild chimps communicate 19 specific messages to one another with a "lexicon" of 66 gestures by following and filming communities of chimps in Uganda's Budongo Forest Reserve, and examining more than 5,000 incidents of these meaningful exchanges.

4. 略

Unit 2

Text A

I.

• What is the database?

The database is <u>a colorful catalog containing reflection signatures of Earth life-forms</u> that might be found on planet surfaces throughout the cosmic hinterlands.

• Why is the database created?

(1) This database gives people the first glimpse at <u>what diverse worlds out there could look like</u>.

(2) It will provide a broader guide, based on Earth life, for the search for surface features of <u>extraterrestrial life</u>.

• Who creates the database?

(1) <u>Lisa Kaltenegger</u> from Cornell University;

(2) <u>Siddharth Hegde</u> of the Max Planck Institute for Astronomy;

(3) <u>Ivan G. Paulino-Lima, Ryan Kent, and Lynn Rothschild</u> from NASA Ames Research Center.

• What does the database include?

(1) It includes <u>reflection signatures</u> of a diversity of <u>pigmented microorganisms</u> isolated from various environments on Earth, including extreme ones.

(2) It includes the cultures of 137 <u>cellular life forms</u>.

• How does the database work?

Astronomers on Earth can see pigmentation on exoplanets and determine <u>their makeup by looking at their color</u>. The database offers a corlorful catalog for astronomers to let them know how they could spot that makeup.

II.

1. c　2. g　3. h　4. j　5. f　6. i　7. d　8. e　9. b　10. a

III.

1. D. 根据文章第二段第一句话,可知原文表达的是"该数据库让我们第一次看到外星球世界有可能是什么样子的",因此选择 D。

2. A. 根据原文第四段段意"科学家们提供的这一数据库包括了地球上生活在极端环境下的极端微生物",并联系上下文得知 inhospitable 在这里的意思为"贫瘠的,不毛的;荒凉的",因此选择 A。

3. B. 根据原文第四、五段可知:地球上许多生命一直由微生物主宰。外星球上的生物可能是从单细胞进化为多细胞的。下一代天文望远镜可以探索外星球上的各种生物。

地球上的天文学家可以通过观测外星球的颜色,并根据它们的颜色来确定其构造。因此,只有 B 选项符合原文信息。

4. B。根据原文第六段可知"在马萨葡萄园岛一个牡蛎塘里获得的卵胞藻",因此选择 B。

5. D。根据原文最后一段可知"此次研究将为今后探索外星球的地貌特征提供一个更广泛的指导",因此选择 D。

Text B

Ⅰ.

1. F. The explosion was 20 times brighter than all the stars in the Milky Way galaxy combined.

根据文章第二段第一句话,可知原文表达的是"此次爆炸所发出的光亮是太阳的 5700 亿倍,是银河系中所有星体总光度的 20 倍",因此题干中"是银河系中大部分星体总光度的 20 倍"是错误的。

2. F. All Sky Automated Survey for Supernovae discovered ASASSN-15lh last June.

根据文章第四段,可知原文意思是"该爆炸和所产生的气体云以该天文学家团队的名称 All Sky Automated Survey for Supernovae 命名为 ASASSN-15lh,该团队于去年 6 月发现了 ASASSN-15lh",因此,题干中"该团队于本周发现了 ASASSN-15lh"的信息是错误的。

3. T。根据文章第五段第一句话,可以肯定"超新星是一种罕见的、通常非常剧烈的现象,它包含了在恒星内部大部分物质的爆炸"。

4. T。根据文章第六段可知"(球状气体)无法用肉眼观测,因为它距离地球有 38 亿光年",因此可判断题干信息正确。

5. F. The astronomers have not defined the object in the middle of the ball of gas yet.

根据文章第七段可知"球状气体中心有一个约 10 英里的物体,天文学家们正在尝试确定该物体的性质"。题干与原文意思不符,因此是错误的。

Ⅱ.

1. It is a rare and often dramatic phenomenon that involves the explosion of most of the material within a star. Supernovas can be very bright for a short time and usually release huge amounts of energy.

2. According to Subo Dong, at this point, the scientists still do not know what could be the power source for ASASSN-15lh.

3. It will help astronomers to settle the question of whether a suprnova truly caused the space explosion and allow astronomers to see the host galaxy surrounding the object in center of the ball of gas.

4. 略

Unit 3

Text A

Ⅰ.

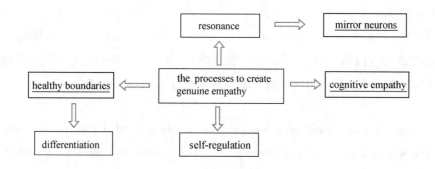

Ⅱ.

1. e 2. f 3. c 4. a 5. d 6. g 7. b

Ⅲ.

1. D. 原文第二段提到:区别于同情,共鸣通常指积极主动地尝试理解他人,产生助人行为,利于社会关系的发展,因此选择 D。

2. A. 原文第三段提到:镜像神经元的存在可以解释"共鸣"。镜像神经元作为人类大脑的组成部分,对他人表达的情感给予反应,然后自身重现相同的情感。这些神经元帮助解释了人们如何以及为什么能够读懂别人的思想并理解他们的感受,因此选择 A。

3. B. 根据原文第五段段意:自我调控是一项重要技能,在了解别人不幸遭遇时,能及时调整自我情绪以免陷入自身的痛苦经历中。例如,当你听说了别人的伤心事,你在理解他人情感的同时不会使自身陷入由于这些情感带来的不良反应中,因此选择 B。

4. D. 根据原文第七段段意:分化是指个体能够将理智与情感区分开的能力,人们的分化能力越好,精神状态恢复就越快,他们的婚姻关系就越健康持久,因此选择 D。

Text B

Ⅰ.

1. F. Regular eye contact is expected in Western societies.

根据文章第二段第一句话,可知原文表达的是"一般在西方,眼神接触是有规律性的,并不是持久不变的"。而题干的信息与原文意思完全相反,因此是错误的。

2. F. The dog will hurt you if you intimidate it with constant eye contact.

根据文章第二段第三句话,可知原文意思是"甚至在人类和非人类之间,有时候持续的眼神接触都是不妥当的。《新西兰医学期刊》曾报道如此多的小孩被宠物狗袭击的一个原因就是他们和宠物之间长时间压制性的眼神接触使宠物感受到威胁而进行自卫",因此题干中"即使你长时间用眼神接触的方式进行恐吓,狗也不会伤害你"的信息是错误的。

3. T. 根据文章第三段段意,可以肯定"在交谈中,当你躲避眼神接触时,你会被认为不诚实或是欺骗,即使因为你是因为害羞或是紧张",因此是正确的。

4. T. 根据文章第六段第三句话,"如果你尝试传递一个严肃的信息,你就不要眨眼睛,练习直接的目光接触,因为限制眨眼次数会增加信息的可信度"。题干与原文意思相符,因此是正确的。

5. F. You can not always keep your eyes in the middle of triangle when talking to others. 根据文章第五段第一句话,可知原文表达的意思是"花太多时间盯着三角区也会传递出不适宜的非语言信息"。而题干的意思与原文意思相反,是错误的。

Ⅱ.

1. Because it is the most immediate and noticeable nonverbal message you can send to others. The self-assurance and confidence conveyed by direct eye contact put both parties at ease within a conversation.

2. They recommend the appropriate amount of eye contact should be a series of long glances instead of intense stares, looking someone in the eye for intervals of four to five seconds, then looking away briefly—in the middle of the triangle—then re-establish eye contact.

3. Yes. Blinking more than the average 6 – 10 times per minute can be a good indicator that a person is attracted to the person they're talking to, and is for this reason used as a sign of flirting.

Unit 4

Text A

Ⅰ.

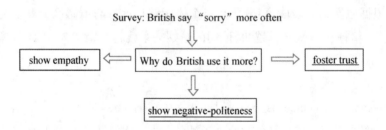

Ⅱ.

1. g 2. d 3. i 4. h 5. c 6. b 7. e 8. a 9. f 10. j

Ⅲ.

1. D. 根据原文第三段和第四段段意可以知道 A 和 C 是正确的,B 是常识。用排除法,因此选择 D。

2. C. 根据原文第四段段意:"我们用这个词来引起共鸣,所以我会说'这雨天真糟糕',英国人和加拿大人就是经常在这种情况下使用'抱歉'这个词,但他们本质上并没有要道歉的意思"可知,大多数情况下,英国人和加拿大人用"抱歉"一词不是要道歉,而是引起共鸣,因此选择 C。

    3. B. 根据原文第五段段意:英国社会注重以不打扰个人空间、不过分关注来表示对他人的尊重,这叫作"间接礼貌手段",因此选择 B。

    4. C. 根据原文第五段段意"美国人的性格是倾向于直接礼貌手段,他们很友好也希望成为团体中的一员",结合选项,因此选择 C。

    5. B. 根据原文第三段段意:英国人说"抱歉"并不代表他们是懊悔的或者是抱歉的,可以确定 A 是错误的;根据第六段段意:英国人在很多情况下使用"抱歉"会让其他人觉得很困扰,接下来文章中提到为了"询问信息"或"希望坐旁边的位置"英国人都用"抱歉"而不是用其他人都使用的"打扰了",可以确定 B 是正确的;根据第七段段意:在"正向礼貌"文化的国家,多使用"抱歉"会让他人困扰,但是同时 Fox 认为多在尊重"逆向礼貌"文化的国家使用"抱歉"并不是坏事。C 选项的内容只适用于有"逆向礼貌"文化的国家,所以 C 是错误的。D 选项在文章中并没有提及。因此,选择 B。

Text B

Ⅰ.

    1. F. Kieren has painted helicopter picking up men and women, snake and crocodile on the mural.

    根据文章第二段,可知 Kieren 只提到了直升机、男人、女人、蛇和鳄鱼。因此题干中给出的"海龟"的信息是错误的。

    2. F. The stall in Darwin sells fabrics, housewares and clothes.

    根据文章第三段,可知这些艺术家售卖的物品中没有提及"画",因此,题干中"画"的信息是错误的。

    3. F. The alarming system is under discussion after the evacuation.

    根据文章第六段最后一句话,可以肯定社区居民提出了设置汽笛以提醒水位的主意,但是这并不是政府已经做了的事情。由此题干中"已经设立了报警机制"的信息是错误的。

    4. F. Flood mitigation works are in plan.

    根据文章第七段第一句话"……正在考虑洪水后的重建工作",而题干的信息是"正在进行重建工作",因此是错误的。

    5. T. 根据文章第九段,可知 Bremner 提到"撤离工作应该以社区为导向",言下之意,她觉得目前的撤离工作太过分散,还需要改善。题干与原文意思相符,是正确的。

Ⅱ.

    1. 略

    2. I could consider setting up the alarming system, building a dam to prevent regular floods, or move the community far from the coast.

    3. Do prevention work before floods, and move to places with higher interior or urge the

government to build a dam.

4. They can do more to attract people's attention to the infrastructure work, like lauching some campaigns.

阅读专业篇

Unit 1

Text A:

Ⅰ.

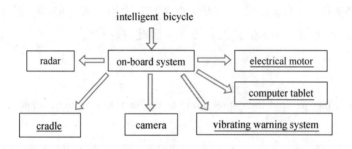

Ⅱ.

1. d 2. c 3. a 4. e 5. b 6. i 7. h 8. j 9. f 10. g

Ⅲ.

1. A. 根据原文第一段段意:荷兰在周一推出了其国内首款"智能自行车"。这种"智能自行车"装有一系列的电子设备,能帮助降低事故发生率。在这个酷爱骑自行车的国家当中,老年骑自行车者事故频发,因此选择 A。

2. C. 根据原文第二段段意:"智能自行车"是由荷兰政府委托荷兰应用科学研究院开发的。这款原型机依靠电力运行,车把下方装有前视雷达,后方挡泥板上装有相机。由此可知,这款原型机是依靠电力运行的,因此选择 C。

3. D. 根据原文第四段段意:测试车的前置和后置检测装备通过机载计算机与振动警报系统相连接。内置在自行车车座和车把中的振动警报系统,能够提醒骑自行车者将可能发生的危险。由此可知,振动警报系统能够提醒自行车可能发生的危险。因此,接近句意的选项为 D。

4. D. 根据原文第六段段意:它还有一个吊架,能够置入平板电脑。该平板电脑能无线上网,以及通过专门应用程序与自行车"对话"。由此可知,选项 A、B、C 都是正确的,因此选择 D。

5. D. 根据原文第八段段意:一位参与该项目的荷兰组织应用科学研究院的人员,莫里斯·科瓦勒纳说道:"事故通常发生在当骑自行车者朝后看或者当被别人快速超车吓到之时。"因此选择 D。

Text B

I.

1. F. Robots will pay more attention to fitting into our homes.

根据文章第二段第一句话,可知原文表达的是"如果未来机器人能成为我们每天生活中的一部分,那么它们需要更适应家庭而不是工厂的地板",因此题干中直接给出"将来机器人将会更加注重适应工业生产"的信息是错误的。

2. F. Roboy doesn't look very endearing at the moment. In fact, it looks more like a cyborg skeleton than a charming child, but it's still a work in progress.

根据文章第四段第一句话,可知原文意思是"现阶段机器小子看起来并不招人喜爱,但它仍在改进之中",因此,题干中"机器小子并不需要改进"的信息是错误的。

3. T. 根据文章第四段最后一句话,可以肯定"赞助商可以拍卖机器人身上的部位作为商标或是雇用机器人将其作为商业目的"。

4. F. Instead of motors in its joints, Roboy uses motor assemblies that pull elastic cables.

根据文章第五段第二句话,可知"机器小子采用是的电动机组合,可以牵引有弹性的线缆进行活动,而不是在关节处安装发动机",而题干的信息与原文意思完全相反,因此是错误的。

5. T. 根据文章第三段,可知"高1.2米的机器小子采用了'软机器人'拘束用来模仿人体机能"。题干与原文意思相符,是正确的。

II.

1. It is to push for the acceptance of service robots by making people more comfortable having them around all the time.

2. Because built out of plastic, it is modeled on the human musculoskeletal system, but this mimicry goes beyond the aesthetic. Instead of motors in its joints, Roboy uses motor assemblies that pull elastic cables, so the system operates in a way similar to muscles and tendons.

3. By sponsorship and crowd funding that includes auctioning space on the robot for logos, and hiring it out for business functions when completed.

4. 略

Unit 2

Text A

I.

Five facts on electric cars:

1. Batteries can go dead just like gas tanks can go empty.

2. Owning an electric car doesn't mean you must own a second car unless you frequently

need to travel long distances.

3. Electric cars tend to be smaller than conventional cars.

4. Electric cars can be pricier than their conventional counterparts.

5. Electric cars have multiple benefits. For example, a quieter ride with less air pollution, less costly to operate, more reliable.

Ⅱ.

1. c 2. f 3. g 4. h 5. e 6. i 7. a 8. j 9. b 10. d

Ⅲ.

1. B. 根据原文第二段段意:就如同汽油箱会空一样电池也会耗尽,而这种情况对预期电动汽车购买者造成了很大程度的焦虑。所以电池会耗尽才是最佳答案,因此选择 B。

2. D. 根据原文第二段段意:通常推荐整夜为电动汽车充电即为满电,尽管有人担忧"快充"没有整夜充那么耐用,但充电站即将开始投放使用,电动汽车只需充20分钟。问题是电动汽车充满电需要多长时间,因此选择 D。

3. C. 根据原文第三段段意:除非你需要经常长距离旅行不然没必要除了电动汽车外再有第二辆车。是否需要第二辆非电动汽车的原因不是其他,而是取决于是否经常性长距离旅行,因此选择 C。

4. D. 根据原文第四段段意:许多电动汽车很小的原因是电池能量密度低,同时还在于重量和车程。前三个选项都是原因之一,因此选择 D。

5. A. 根据原文第五段段意:有些人提出电动汽车应该比传统汽车定价更低,因为基于等价的生产基础,它们只用更少的零件便能更便宜地被制造出来。电费和汽油费都不是电动汽车定价的关键,而是取决于制造汽车时使用零件的多少,因此选择 A。

Text B

Ⅰ.

1. T. 根据文章第一段可知,加州大学戴维斯分校的研究表明有1/3到大约60%的加州电动汽车的购买主要是源于单人驾车可使用偶尔堵塞的高乘载车辆车道,因此题干的大约30%到60%是正确的。

2. F. As a leader of accepting PEV, California uses carrot-and-stick approach of incentives and perks have long included stickers that give alternative-energy car buyers access to (usually) less congestad lanes.

根据文章第二段可知,在电动汽车接纳方面加州是领先者,政府决策者采取软硬兼施的激励和额外补贴的办法来推广电动汽车的使用,因此题干只提到奖励办法是不全面的。

3. F. In the more densely congested Bay Area and Los Angeles, HOV access as the main purchase motivation is higher than in other regions.

在文章第八段第一句中,"more densely congested Bay Area"指的是更密集拥堵的旧金山湾区,而不是所有旧金山湾区,题干表述不恰当。

4. T. 根据文章第九段可知,研究确认超过80%的电动汽车用于上下班通勤,而纯电动汽车的通勤率低于插电式混合动力汽车,因此题干与原文表述一致。

5. F. There is an assumption that the effectiveness of this benefit could be increased by prioritizing PHEVs with larger all-electric range and not to just any PHEV.

根据文章最后一段可知,据假设称主要是通过拥有更长电气化车程的混合动力车来增加这种益处的效率,而不是任何一种短距离车程的混合动力车,因此题干表述太片面。

Ⅱ.

1. HOV access is the key for California plug-in car purchases.

2. They adopt a carrot-and-stick approach of incentives and perks have long included stickers that give alternative-energy car buyers access to (usually) less congested lanes.

3. Because time is money to them, so saving minutes on busy freeways is a motivator.

4. 略

Unit 3

Text A

Ⅰ.

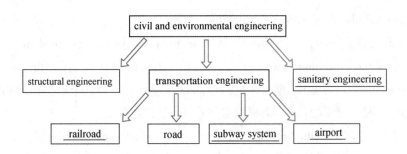

Ⅱ.

1. h 2. d 3. a 4. e 5. j 6. b 7. i 8. f 9. c 10. g

Ⅲ.

1. D. 原文第一段提到土木工程学研究建筑环境。第二段又谈到土木工程下分三大类:结构工程学(structural engineering)、交通工程学(transportation engineering)和卫生工程学(sanitary engineering)。A、B、C 选项都不完整,因此选择 D。

2. A. 根据原文第一段内容可知:由于发展了清洁水的供给和卫生系统,土木工程比历史上所有的医生拯救的生命都多,因此选择 A。

3. C. 根据原文第二段段意:建筑是土木工程最显而易见的成果,相比而言,给水排水这些卫生工程则不怎么醒目。因此,选项为 C。

4. C. 根据原文第二段段意:土木工程下分三大类:结构工程学(structural engineering)、交通工程学(transportation engineering)和卫生工程学(sanitary engineering),因此选择 C。

5. A. 根据原文第三段段意：土木工程可以运用于很多领域：建筑、桥梁、航空航天、汽车、轮船和电力等工业。只要涉及建筑设施的就有运用土木工程的地方，因此，选择 A。

Text B

Ⅰ.

1. F. The main part of the Villa Savoye (living-room, kitchen, bedrooms and bathrooms) is located on the first floor.

根据文章第一部分"Introduction"第一段"The main part of the house (living-room, kitchen, bedrooms and bathrooms) is located on the first floor"，可知萨伏伊别墅的主体部分，即客厅、厨房、卧室和浴室都在二楼。在英式英语里 the ground floor 指紧贴地面的那个楼层。它上面的一层叫作 the first floor。因此题干中直接给出"萨伏伊别墅的主体部分，即客厅、厨房、卧室和浴室都在一楼"的信息是错误的。

2. T. 根据文章"Introduction"第一段"There is also a garage capable of storing 3 automobiles of the time on the ground floor, which was a milestone in the history of architecture and a great step forward for its time"，可以肯定萨伏伊别墅是建筑史的里程碑，是它那个时代的一个大进步。

3. F. Le Corbusier's concept of the "machine as a home" means that the functions of everyday life inside become criticoal to architecture design.

从文章第二部分"Concept"的第一句话"The Villa Savoye was designed by Le Corbusier as a paradigm of the 'machine as a home', so that the functions of everyday life inside become critical to its design"可以知道，勒科尔比西埃的设计理念是以日常家居生活的功能作为建筑设计的核心，因而题干的信息"把机器当作房子"是错误的。

4. T. 根据文章"Introduction"第三段第一句"The house was inhabited by its owners for a short period of time"以及第四段内容，可以肯定萨伏伊别墅原本是私人住宅，而现在已经成为一座博物馆，每年接待成千上万的游客。题干的信息与原文意思一致，是正确的。

5. T. 根据文章第二部分"Concept"第二段"Architecture followed the style of airplanes, cars and ships, with the declared aim of achieving mass production of housing"，可知"建筑可以像制造飞机、轿车和轮船一样，能够批量地生产住宅"。题干与原文意思相符，是正确的。

Ⅱ.

1. It is located in the suburb of Paris, which is less than one hour's drive from the capital.

2. Because there is a garage on the ground floor capable of storing 3 automobiles of the time.

3. It stresses that architecture design should consider the needs of daily life for people living in it.

4. 略

Unit 4

Text A

I.

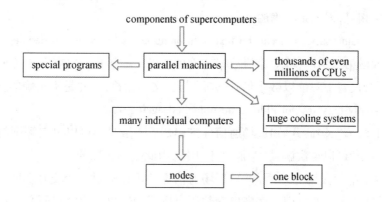

II.

1. e 2. h 3. a 4. b 5. d 6. c 7. j 8. f 9. g 10. i

III.

1. C. 根据第三段的内容,B 选项是最初的超级计算机的 CPU 情况,D 选项是个干扰项,根据 Andrew Grimshaw 教授的解释可知,C 选项符合中国的天河二号超级计算机的情况;而 A 选项根据常识即可排除。

2. D. 根据第三段的内容,超级计算机的特点有耗能大、产热能多和需要庞大的冷却系统;因此 A、B、C 三个选项都是其特点之一,所以 D 选项"以上都是"是正确选项。

3. B. 题干询问虚拟超级计算机如何创建。根据第五段的内容,虚拟超级计算机可以通过各个单机进行计算机网络体系构建而创建。A 选项是连接一些计算机,C 选项是连接一些平行机,D 选项是几个平行机的网络体系构建,这 3 个选项均存在概念表述不准确的问题,因此均不可入选。

4. A. 题干询问为什么虚拟超级计算机容易运行。根据第六段第一句的解释:在虚拟超级计算机上运行那些很简单。因为每个问题都相互独立,我可以将这些工作分散到各个地方进行。所以 A 选项是正确答案,B 选项是一个强干扰项,与 A 选项比起来,B 选项具有片面性,而 C、D 选项均不够准确。

5. C. 根据最后两段 Professor Grimshaw 的解释,他对于未来超级计算机在科学研究中的功用是持积极肯定态度的,因此 C 选项是正确答案。

Text B

I.

1. F. Barclays use the contact-less payment system for payments under £15 by allowing visa cards to be placed near the payment pad.

根据文章第二段第二句话,可知文中表达的是"巴克莱银行使用类似的支付系统允许签证置于附近的支付平板电脑上支付15英镑以下的金额";而题干中给出的是"支付15英镑以上的金额",与原文意思相违背,因此是错误的。

2. T. 根据文中第三段第一句话可知,手机用户如果发现手机丢失,可以远程拭接手机擦除掉手机即时支付等信息,这样以防止一些个人财务支付信息泄露等安全问题。题干意思与原文相符,因此是正确的。

3. F. The data transferred can be text data or numbers between two devices.

根据第六段第二句话,可知通信数据传输可以以文本形式或数字形式传输,因此题干中给出"在两个设备上只能以数字形式传输"与原文不相符,因此是不正确的。

4. F. Usually tags are not able to be unlocked again.

根据第七段第二句话,可知近场通信标签锁住后一般是不可以再次解锁的,因此题干中给出"标签通常可以再次解锁"与原文不相符,因此是不正确的。

5. T. 根据第七段第三句话,可知近场通信标签可以通过一个支持NFC的手机来对其编码,然后选择合适的应用程序来启动编码。题干中给出的内容与原文意思相符,因此是正确的。

Ⅱ.

1. With these tags they can download information from film posters, read a recipe from an advertisement, and select university curriculum timetable and so much more.

2. If someone loses his mobile phone, he can have it wiped remotely as soon as he notices it is missing. This combats some security issues regarding instant phone payments.

3. They can be locked so that any data stored on them cannot then be changed. Usually tags are not able to be unlocked again, making them more secure.

4. 略

Unit 5

Text A

Ⅰ.

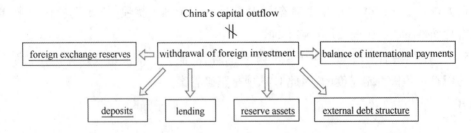

Ⅱ.

1. d 2. i 3. e 4. b 5. g 6. c 7. h 8. j 9. a 10. f

Ⅲ.

1. D. 根据原文第二段段意:(资金)流出发生在国内银行和企业大力增加海外资产

的股份和还债方面,可知 A、B、C 3 个选项都是正确的,D 不是中国资金流出的原因,因此选择 D。

2. C. 根据原文第四段段意:在去年的前三个季度,中国的海外资产增加了 2727 亿美元。C 选项符合题意,因此选择 C。

3. A. 根据原文第二段段意:(资金)流出发生在国内银行和企业大力增加海外资产的股份和还债方面,可知 A 正确。第三段段意:外汇管理局说:"(资金流出)和所谓的外国资金有很大的区别",所以 B 选项错。根据第五段段意:中国海外净财政资产位居世界第二,所以选项 C 错误。因此,正确的选项为 A。

4. C. 根据原文倒数第二段段意:中国报道称当前的账户余额已从第三季度的 603 亿美元上涨到了第四季度的 843 亿美元。由此可知,第四季度的账户余额比第三季度增加了 240 亿美元,因此选择 C。

5. B. 根据原文第六段段意:到 2015 年年底为止,中国的外汇储备下降至 3.3 万亿美元,但仍然是世界上最大的,因此选择 B。

Text B

Ⅰ.

1. T. 根据文章第三段第一句话的含义:经济合作和发展组织在星期四表达了对全球经济的关心。题干与原文意思相符,是正确的。

2. F. Lloyds Banking Group and Barclays, along with Credit Suisse, are laying off workers in the UK.

根据文章第四段第一句话,可知原文意思是"劳埃德银行集团、巴克莱银行和瑞士信贷正在英国裁员"。因此,题干中"在美国裁员"的信息是错误的。

3. F. The British gas owner, Centrica, reiterated on Thursday that it is to axe 1,000 jobs in the UK this year.

根据文章第四段最后一句话,可知原文的意思是"英国燃气公司森特理克在周四重申今年在英国将裁员 1000 人,达到 2020 年裁员 4000 人的一部分"。而题干的信息与原文意思完全相反,因此是错误的。

4. F. According to Michael Hewson, consumption rates will be affected by the recovery in the UK.

根据文章第五段最后一句话,"很多英国经济复苏都是建立在消费基础上的,所以,最终将影响消费率"。而题干的信息与原文意思完全相反,因此是错误的。

5. F. Wages excluding bonuses had risen by 2% year-on-year at the end of 2015.

根据最后一段,可知"工资扣除奖金在 2015 年年末同比上升了 2%"。题干中的"工资同比上升了 2%"是错误的。

II.

1. Factories, the high street, banking, media and energy can be affected by job losses.
2. Because of the collapse in crude prices, which has hit oil companies hard.
3. They are likely to affect the buy-to-let market and the wider housing market.
4. 略

Unit 6

Text A

I.

1. outdoor air pollutants
2. faulty boilers
3. open fires
4. fly sprays
5. air freshers
6. cooking appliances
7. personal hygiene
8. cleaning products
9. furniture
10. furnishings
11. glue and insulation
12. particulates
13. nitrogen oxides
14. formaldehyde vapour
15. lung and kidney development
16. miscarriage
17. hearts attacks
18. diabetes
19. dementia
20. obesity

II.

1. d 2. e 3. a 4. f 5. g 6. b 7. c 8. j 9. h 10. i

III.

1. B. 根据原文第一段最后一句:虽然近年来室外空气污染的危害已得到很好的证明,但是更多的危害实际来自家庭秘密杀手。再结合第一句,可以推断出这些秘密杀手是日常物件及用具,故正确选项为 B。

2. D. 根据原文第二段第一句:这将警示人们日常使用的厨房用品,有损坏的锅炉、明火、蚊虫喷雾剂,甚至是空气清新剂,都会导致室内空气质量的不良。可知 A、B、C 选项都有,故选 D。

3. A. 根据原文第四段第一句判断,很明显选项 A 正确。

4. A. 根据原文第五段第一句可知需要采取更多措施限制排污者,保护公众免受有害释放物的伤害,尤其是在城区及靠近学校区域,因此选择 A。

5. D. 该题的关键词是 force,掌握这一线索,答案很明显。根据原文第五段段意:为了治理污染,需要采取很多措施,如通过当地权威机构、更严格的立法等。但是要 force(迫使)排污者减少有害物质排放,关键在于更严格的立法,因此选择 D。

Text B

I.

1. T. 根据文章第二段第一句话,可知由于空间有限,在该公司某些区域不能完成自重供料。题干与原文意思相符,是正确的。

2. T. 根据文章第二段最后一句话,可知新型大型袋式卸货机不仅能减少劳动力,还能减少粉尘排放,安装在既定位置非常合适。因此,题干正确。

3. F. Previously operators handled 32 bags mannally each eight-hour day.

根据文章第三段最后一句话,可以推断出袋式卸货机只是在工作日才使用,所以题干中的 each day 错误。

4. T. 根据文章第四段可以推断出由于空间有限,且顶高不够,所以没有足够空间装置袋式卸货机,故题干内容正确。

5. F. In order to avoid relocating the knife gate valves and chutes, the bulk bag discharger needs to be installed.

根据文章第五段第二句,可知新型袋式卸货机能成功避免重装刀型进模口阀门和斜槽,题干与原文意思相反,错误。

II.

1. Because the company intends to improve productivity and working conditions. And the newest bulk bag chargeres can enhance labor efficiency and reduce dust.

2. The discharger holds two bulk bags side-by-side that provide enough starch to keep the line running for two or more days. Once a bag is hoisted into position, an operator pulls the bag spout over a clamp ring to create a secure, dust-tight connection between the clean side of the bag spout and the clean side of a telescoping tube. As the bag empties and elongates, the telescoping tube maintains constant downward tension, promoting complete discharge.

3. The newest bulk bag discharger is a twin half-frame unit that handles two types of starch in a small space on the plant's fourth floor and it can keep the line running for two or more days. The equipment discharges through two outlets spaced closely enough to avoid relocating the knife gate valves and chutes, while the low profile design saves 4 in. of headroom. While the old one had 55-lb. bags of starch from the third to the fourth floor. And the bags needed to be handled manually each eight-hour day. This equipment required more headroom above the units to use a forklift for loading and removing bulk bags.

4. 略

Unit 7

Text A

I.

1. sculptor
2. *The Florence Pieta*
3. design Julius' own tomb
4. a sculpture of Moses
5. the fresco in the Sistine Chapel
6. artist
7. *The Last Judgment*
8. altar
9. 89
10. numberless unsurpassable works of art

II.

1. h 2. c 3. b 4. a 5. d 6. g 7. e 8. i 9. j 10. f

III.

1. B. 根据原文第二段,米开朗琪罗父亲是当地治安官,而不是米开朗琪罗是治安官,A 错。第二段提到了米开朗琪罗出生后不久去佛罗伦萨,所以不是在佛罗伦萨出生的,C 错。D 说米开朗琪罗是许多艺术家的赞助人,文章根本没提及,不符合实情,D 错。而段末提到他住到艺术家赞助人洛伦佐·德·美第奇家,因此选择 B。

2. C. 根据原文第三段最后一句话可知米开朗琪罗早年主要做雕刻,因此选择 C。

3. A. 根据原文第四段最后一句话可知《哀悼基督》让米开朗琪罗功成名就,回到佛罗伦萨时已经是位出名的雕塑家,所以正确选项为 A。选项 B"这一雕刻让米开朗琪罗健康快乐",但原文提到雕刻时他有时痛得无法工作,与原文意思相悖。选项 C 说他逃回佛罗伦萨,也与原文冲突。选项 D 说他完成《哀悼基督》后就无法工作,根据下文,可知并非实情。

4. D. 题目问的是为何米开朗琪罗没有完成为 Julius 设计陵墓的工作。从文章第五段可知,原因是二人的争吵及项目耗时,因此选择 D。

5. D 从文章第七段和第八段可知,米开朗琪罗在西斯廷教堂完成了天顶壁画和神坛画《末日审判》,因此选择 D。

Text B

I.

1. F. Chanel's LBD was simple, with only diagonal pin tucks as decoration.

根据文章第一段可知,原文说的"小黑裙"非常简洁,只有些斜细褶皱作为装饰,并非奢华花哨。因此题干的信息是错误的。

2. F. The LBD was first introduced by Chanel but Audrey Hepburn's LBD was designed by Givenchy.

根据文章第二段可知,赫本的小黑裙由纪梵希设计。因此,题干说由香奈儿设计的信息是错误的。

3. T. 根据文章第三段第一句话可知,"香奈儿预见小黑裙会成为女士们下午茶和晚宴的新服装",再根据下文提到小黑裙的受欢迎程度,可知她是预想成真了。

4. F. Chanel was the champion of beige and neutral. She didn't like Poiret's taste of fashion.

根据文章第四段第一、二句:香奈儿,这位最擅用米黄色和素净色的设计师,自从在歌剧晚会上看到普瓦雷设计的色彩艳丽、纷繁撞色的服装,就决定改变时尚领域。而题干的信息与原文意思完全相反,因此是错误的。

5. T.

根据文章倒数第二段可知,香奈儿有时尚远见,能凭直觉预测时尚界的走势,知道女人们想要什么。题干信息与原文意思相符,是正确的。

Ⅱ.

1. She wants her LBD not to show stains and to fit every woman. The dress is simple yet sexy.

2. Her LBD is radically simple, well-cut, elegant, soft, impressive and sexy.

3. In the clothes she wore daily, a woman no longer had to create the impression of great wealth. In other words, women preferred simple dress that made them comfortable and able to work easily.

4. 略

Glossary

A

academic	/ˌækəˈdemɪk/	adj.	学科的,学术的
accessory	/əkˈsesəri/	n.	配件
activator	/ˈæktɪveɪtə/	n.	催化剂,触媒剂
aerospace	/ˈeərəʊspeɪs/	n.	航空与航天
affinity	/əˈfɪnəti/	n.	密切关系
allegedly	/əˈledʒɪdli/	adv.	据说
all-electric	/ˈɔːlɪˈlektrɪk/	adj.	全电气化的
altar	/ˈɔːltə(r)/	n.	祭坛,圣坛;圣餐台
alternative	/ɔːlˈtɜːnətɪv/	n.	二中选一;供替代的选择
architect	/ˈɑːkɪtekt/	n.	建筑师
arguably	/ˈɑːgjuəbli/	adv.	可论证地
asthma	/ˈæsmə/	n.	哮喘
auction	/ˈɔːkʃən/	v.	竞卖,拍卖
austerity	/ɒˈsterəti/	n.	简朴,朴素;节衣缩食
authoritative	/ɔːˈθɒrətətɪv/	adj.	权威的;有权利的
autonomous	/ɔːˈtɒnəməs/	adj.	有自主权的
axe	/æks/	vt.	大量削减
a host of			许多,大量
advance wave upon wave			前赴后继
air freshener			空气清新剂
TNO			应用科学研究院
architectural heritage			建筑遗产
at the forefront of			处于最前列

Glossary

B

battery	/ˈbætri/	n.	电池,蓄电池
beige	/beɪʒ/	n.	米黄色;淡棕色
blast	/blɑːst/	n.	爆炸
bulk	/bʌlk/	n.	体积;大块
bumper	/ˈbʌmpə(r)/	n.	保险杠
be equated with			等同于
BEVs (battery electric vehicles)			纯电动汽车
buy-to-let			购房出租

C

carrot-and-stick	/ˌkærətənˈstɪk/	adj.	威逼加利诱的;软硬兼施的
carve	/kɑːv/	vt.	切开;雕刻
cast	/kɑːst/	vt.	投射
catalog	/ˈkætəlɔːg/	n.	目录;目录册,目录簿
charge	/tʃɑːdʒ/	n.	电荷
chassis	/ˈʃæsi/	n.	(车辆的)底盘
chic	/ʃiːk/	n.	高雅,雅致
chimpanzee	/ˌtʃɪmpænˈziː/	n.	黑猩猩
chute	/ʃuːt/	n.	斜槽,滑道
clamp	/klæmp/	n.	钳,压板
clashing	/ˈklæʃɪŋ/	adj.	不相容的,相冲突的
clipping	/ˈklɪpɪŋ/	n.	修剪;剪掉
clue	/kluː/	n.	线索;提示
collapse	/kəˈlæps/	n.	(突然)降价,贬值;暴跌
combat	/ˈkɒmbæt/	vt.	防止
commission	/kəˈmɪʃən/	vt.	任命;正式委托
commute	/kəˈmjuːt/	vi.	乘公交车上下班
compelling	/kəmˈpelɪŋ/	adj.	非常强烈的;不可抗拒的
concrete	/ˈkɒnkriːt/	n.	混凝土
congested	/kənˈdʒestɪd/	adj.	拥挤的;堵塞的
convent	/ˈkɒnvənt/	n.	女修道院

conventional	/kənˈvenʃənl/	adj.	传统的；平常的
convey	/kənˈveɪ/	v.	传达；运送；表达
coordinated	/kəʊˈɔːdɪneɪtɪd/	adj.	协调的
counterpart	/ˈkaʊntəpɑːt/	n.	配对物；极相似的人或物
couturier	/kuˈtjʊərieɪ/	n.	女裁缝师，女服设计师
cradle	/ˈkreɪdl/	n.	吊架，支架，吊篮
crashworthiness	/ˈkræʃwɜːðɪnəs/	n.	防撞性
crucial	/ˈkruːʃl/	adj.	关键性的；决定性的
crude	/kruːd/	n.	原油
crystallize	/ˈkrɪstəlaɪz/	v.	结晶；（使想法、信仰等）明确
cyborg	/ˈsaɪbɔːg/	n.	半人半机器的电物
capital flow			资本流动
carbon monoxide			一氧化碳
cast a shadow			蒙上一层阴影
change of heart			改变心意；改变看法
Church of St Peter's			圣彼得教堂
cognitive empathy			认知移情
coincide with			与……一致，与……相符
combustion engine			内燃机
computer tablet			平板电脑
cooling system			冷却系统
crack down			采取严厉措施，镇压
crowd funding			群众集资

D

dander	/ˈdændə/	n.	皮屑
database	/ˈdeɪtəbeɪs/	n.	数据库，资料库，信息库
decal	/ˈdiːkæl/	n.	贴花纸
deficit	/ˈdefɪsɪt/	n.	缺陷；赤字；亏空
de luxe	/ˌdəˈlʌks/	adj.	高级的；豪华的
dementia	/dɪˈmenʃə/	n.	痴呆
density	/ˈdensəti/	n.	密度
deposit	/dɪˈpɒzɪt/	n.	储蓄，存款；保证金

Glossary

depreciation	/dɪˌpriːʃɪˈeɪʃən/	n.	货币贬值;跌价;(资产等)折旧
devalue	/ˌdiːˈvæljuː/	vt.	贬低
devastating	/ˈdevəsteɪtɪŋ/	adj.	灾难性的
diabetes	/ˌdaɪəˈbiːtiːz/	n.	糖尿病
diagonal	/daɪˈægənl/	adj.	斜线的;斜的;斜纹的
discharger	/dɪsˈtʃɑːdʒə/	n.	卸货人
discipline	/ˈdɪsəplɪn/	n.	学科
disclosure	/dɪsˈkləʊʒə(r)/	n.	揭露
downright	/ˈdaʊnraɪt/	adv.	完全地,彻底地
digital information			数字信息
digital signature			数字签名
down time			停机时间
dump into			倒入

E

elongate	/ˈiːlɒŋgeɪt/	v.	延长,加长
empathy	/ˈempəθi/	n.	同感;共鸣;同情
encode	/ɪnˈkəʊd/	v.	编码
encompasse	/ɪnˈkʌmpəs/	vt.	包含,包括
endearing	/ɪnˈdɪərɪŋ/	adj.	令人爱慕的;惹人喜爱的
envision	/ɪnˈvɪʒn/	vt.	想象,预见,展望
epitome	/ɪˈpɪtəmi/	n.	典型;典范
equivalent	/ɪˈkwɪvələnt/	adj.	等价的,相等的
evacuate	/ɪˈvækjueɪt/	vt.	疏散,撤离
exasperate	/ɪgˈzæspəreɪt/	vt.	使恼怒;使恶化
excavate	/ˈekskəveɪt/	vt.	挖掘;开凿
execute	/ˈeksɪkjuːt/	vt.	执行
exoplanet	/ekˈsɒplænɪt/	n.	外星球
explosion	/ɪkˈspləʊʒn/	n.	爆发,爆炸,炸裂
extraterrestrial	/ˌekstrətəˈrestriəl/	adj.	地球外的;外星球的;宇宙的
extremophile	/eksˈtreməˌfaɪ/	n.	极端微生物,极端生物;族群
elastic cable			弹性电缆
elicit one's attention			吸引某人注意

EV			电动汽车
evolutionary biologist			进化生物学家

F

facade	/fə'sɑːd/	n.	（尤指大型建筑物的）正面，临街的一面
faucet	/'fɔːsɪt/	n.	水龙头
fleck	/flek/	n.	微粒，斑点
flirt	/flɜːt/	vi.	调情
foetus	/'fiːtəs/	n.	胎儿
forex	/'fɔːeks/	n.	[经] 外汇
forklift	/'fɔːklɪft/	n.	铲车，叉式升降机
formaldehyde	/fɔː'mældɪhaɪd/	n.	甲醛
foster	/'fɒstə(r)/	vt.	培养；促进
fresco	/'freskəʊ/	n.	壁画
family of origin			原生家庭
fill the gap			填补空白；弥补缺陷
fit into			适合，适应
fly spray			蚊虫喷雾剂
foreign exchange reserve			外汇储备

G

galaxy	/'gæləksi/	n.	星系，银河系
gesture	/'dʒestʃə(r)/	n.	手势；姿势
Givenchy	/dʒɪ'vɑŋʃɪ/	n.	纪梵希（法国时装品牌）
glamorous	/'glæmərəs/	adj.	富有魅力的；迷人的
grid	/grɪd/	n.	格子，格栅
gas tank			汽车油箱

H

haute couture	/ˌəʊt kuˈtjʊə(r)/	n.	高级女式时装
humanoid	/'hjuːmənɔɪd/	n.	仿真机器人；类人动物
hygiene	/'haɪdʒiːn/	n.	卫生
half-frame			半幅，半框

hard evidence			真凭实据
healthy boundary			健康界线
high occupancy vehicle (HOV)			高乘载汽车
hybrid car			混合动力车;双动力汽车
hydroelectric dam			水电站坝

I

imitation	/ˌɪmɪˈteɪʃən/	n.	模仿;仿制品
impassion	/ɪmˈpæʃən/	vt.	激起热情
impending	/ɪmˈpendɪŋ/	adj.	即将发生的
impose	/ɪmˈpəʊz/	v.	施加影响,迫使
incentive	/ɪnˈsentɪv/	n.	动机;刺激
inhabit	/ɪnˈhæbɪt/	vt.	居住于
instant	/ˈɪnstənt/	adj.	即时的
instinctive	/ɪnˈstɪŋktɪv/	adj.	本能的
intelligent bicycle			智能自行车
interdisciplinary	/ˌɪntəˈdɪsəplɪnəri/	adj.	跨学科的,多学科的
interval	/ˈɪntəvl/	n.	间隔
intimidation	/ɪnˌtɪmɪˈdeɪʃn/	n.	恐吓
inundate	/ˈɪnʌndeɪt/	vt.	淹没
invasion	/ɪnˈveɪʒn/	n.	侵犯
invert	/ɪnˈvɜːt/	vt.	使反转
Inherently Low Emission Vehicles (ILEVs)			固有低排放车辆

J

jetliner	/ˈdʒetlaɪnə(r)/	n.	喷气客机

L

lane	/leɪn/	n.	车道;航线
lessor	/leˈsɔː(r)/	n.	出租人
lexicon	/ˈleksɪkən/	n.	词典;专门词汇
lay off			暂时解雇,裁员
lb		abbr.	磅

Le Corbusier			勒科尔比西埃(1887—1965,旅居法国的瑞士建筑设计师)

M

magistrate	/ˈmædʒɪstreɪt/	n.	地方法官,治安官;文职官员
magnetar	/ˈmæɡnɪtɑː/	n.	(有很强磁场的)中子星
masterful	/ˈmɑːstəfl/	adj.	熟练的;娴熟的
Medici Chapel		n.	美第奇教堂
microbial	/maɪˈkrəʊbiəl/	adj.	微生物的,由细菌引起的
microchip	/ˈmaɪkrəʊtʃɪp/	n.	微晶片
microorganism	/ˌmaɪkrəʊˈɔːɡənɪzəm/	n.	微生物
microprocessor	/ˌmaɪkrəʊˈprəʊsesə(r)/	n.	微处理器
milestone	/ˈmaɪlstəʊn/	n.	里程碑
millisecond	/ˈmɪlisekənd/	n.	毫秒
mimic	/ˈmɪmɪk/	vt.	模仿
miscarriage	/ˈmɪskærɪdʒ/	n.	流产,早产
mite	/maɪt/	n.	螨虫
mitigation	/ˌmɪtɪˈɡeɪʃən/	n.	缓解,减轻
Monsieur	/məˈsjɜː/	n.	先生(对法国男性的尊称)
monument	/ˈmɒnjumənt/	n.	纪念碑;遗迹;遗址;丰碑
morale	/məˈrɑːl/	n.	士气
Moses	/ˈməʊzɪz/	n.	摩西(《圣经》故事中犹太人古代领袖)
mould	/məʊld/	n.	霉
mourn	/mɔːn/	vi.	哀悼;哀痛
mudguard	/ˈmʌdɡɑːd/	n.	(自行车)挡泥板
mural	/ˈmjʊərəl/	n.	(大型)壁画
musculoskeletal	/ˌmʌskjʊləʊˈskelətəl/	adj.	肌(与)骨骼的
mathematical calculation			数学计算
Milky Way			银河
mirror neuron			镜像神经元
model on			仿照……制作

N

net	/net/	adj.	净的;净得的;最后的
neurological	/ˌnjʊərəˈlɒdʒɪkl/	adj.	神经的
neutral	/ˈnjuːtrəl/	n.	素净色
niche	/nɪtʃ/	n.	生态位(一个生物所占据的生境的最小单位)
node	/nəʊd/	n.	节点
non-verbal	/ˌnɑːnˈvɜːbl/	adj.	不使用语言的;非语言交际的
natural selection			自然选择;物竞天择
nitrogen oxide			氮氧化合物

O

obesity	/əʊˈbiːsəti/	n.	肥胖症
occupy	/ˈɒkjupaɪ/	vt.	占用
on-board	/ˌɒnˈbɔːd/	adj.	随车携带的
ongoing	/ˈɒngəʊɪŋ/	adj.	不间断的
orphanage	/ˈɔːfənɪdʒ/	n.	孤儿院;孤儿身份
orthogonal	/ɔːˈθɒgənl/	adj.	直角的
overdressed	/ˌəʊvəˈdrest/	adj.	穿着过于正经的,打扮过度的
on-board system			车载系统
open fire			明火

P

paradigm	/ˈpærədaɪm/	n.	范例,样式
parallel machine			并行计算机
particulate	/pɑːˈtɪkjələt/	n.	微粒
patrol	/pəˈtrəʊl/	n.	巡逻
patron	/ˈpeɪtrən/	n.	赞助人,资助人
peculiar	/pɪˈkjuːliə(r)/	adj.	特有的
per se	/ˌpɜːˈseɪ/	adv.	本质上
perk	/pɜːk/	n.	额外补贴
persistent	/pəˈsɪstənt/	adj.	持续的
petaflop	/ˈpetəflɒp/		千万亿次
pieta	/pjeɪˈtɑː/	n.	圣母怜子图,圣母怜子像(雕刻)

pigmentation	/ˌpɪgmenˈteɪʃn/	n.	天然颜色；色素沉着
pigmented	/pɪgˈmentɪd/	adj.	天然色的；本色的
pillar	/ˈpɪlə(r)/	n.	柱，台柱
pin tuck	/ˈpɪnˌtʌk/	n.	细缝儿，细褶儿
pneumatic	/njuːˈmætɪk/	adj.	充气的；气动的
Poissy		n.	（法国）普瓦西
polarize	/ˈpəʊləraɪz/	vt.	使两极化
pope	/pəʊp/	n.	（罗马天主教的）教皇
pop-up	/ˈpɒpˌʌp/	adj.	弹起的
postulate	/ˈpɒstjuleɪt/	vt.	假定
predesigned	/priːdɪˈzaɪnd/	adj.	预先设定的
privacy	/ˈprɪvəsi/	n.	隐私
profile	/ˈprəʊfaɪl/	n.	侧面，半面；外形，轮廓
propel	/prəˈpel/	vt.	推进
prospective	/prəˈspektɪv/	adj.	未来的；预期的
prototype	/ˈprəʊtətaɪp/	n.	原型
provincial	/prəˈvɪnʃl/	adj.	乡下的；外地人的；粗野的
PHEV (plug-in hybrid electric vehicle)			插电式混合动力汽车
plug in			插入（电源）
plug-in vehicle (PEV)			电动汽车
psychology and neuroscience			心理学和神经科学
push the envelope			挑战极限

Q

quadrillion	/kwɒˈdrɪljən/	n.	千的五次方，百万的四次方

R

radar	/ˈreɪdɑː(r)/	n.	雷达
rank second			位列第二
rear	/rɪə(r)/	adj.	后方的
rebate	/ˈriːbeɪt/	n.	折扣
recession	/rɪˈseʃn/	n.	经济衰退，不景气

recipe	/ˈresəpi/	n.	食谱
reiterate	/riˈɪtəreɪt/	vt.	重申；反复地做
remnant	/ˈremnənt/	n.	剩余部分
remorseful	/rɪˈmɔːsfl/	adj.	懊悔的
remotely	/rɪˈməʊtli/	adv.	遥远地
Renaissance	/rɪˈneɪsns/	n.	文艺复兴；文艺复兴时期
resilient	/rɪˈzɪliənt/	adj.	恢复快的
resonance	/ˈrezənəns/	n.	共鸣
rotational	/rəʊˈteɪʃənl/	adj.	转动的
reflection signature			反射特征
reserve asset			储备资产
rigid auger			刚性钻

S

saddle	/ˈsædl/	n.	车座
scatter	/ˈskætə(r)/	vt.	分散
sceptical	/ˈskeptɪkl/	adj.	怀疑的
screw	/skruː/	n.	螺丝钉；螺旋桨
sculptor	/ˈskʌlptə(r)/	n.	雕刻家，雕塑家
sculpture	/ˈskʌlptʃə(r)/	n.	雕刻术；塑像；雕刻品
self-assurance	/ˌselfəˈʃʊərəns/	n.	自信
self-regulation	/ˈselfˌreɡjuˈleɪʃən/	n.	自我调控
semi-permeable	/ˌsemiˈpɜːmiəbl/	adj.	半渗透的
shrink	/ʃrɪŋk/	vi.	(经济)萎缩
silhouette	/ˌsɪluˈet/	n.	服装轮廓
simulate	/ˈsɪmjuleɪt/	vt.	模拟
Sistine Chapel		n.	(罗马梵蒂冈的)西斯廷教堂
slash-necked	/ˈslæʃ nekt/	adj.	斜线颈的
sophisticated	/səˈfɪstɪkeɪtɪd/	adj.	复杂的；精致的；老于世故的
spawn	/spɔːn/	v.	引起
speculation	/ˌspekjuˈleɪʃən/	n.	推断
stain	/steɪn/	n.	污迹；污渍
stall	/stɔːl/	n.	货摊

starch	/stɑːtʃ/	n.	淀粉,含淀粉的食物
sticker	/ˈstɪkə(r)/	n.	粘贴物
stroke	/strəʊk/	n.	中风
subconsciously	/ˌsʌbˈkɒnʃəsli/	adv.	潜意识地
submerge	/səbˈmɜːdʒ/	v.	淹没;沉浸
subtle	/ˈsʌtl/	adj.	微妙的;敏感的;巧妙的
summon	/ˈsʌmən/	vt.	传唤,召唤
superfluous	/suːˈpɜːfluəs/	adj.	过多的
supermassive	/ˈsjuːpəmæsɪv/	adj.	特大质量的
supernova	/ˌsuːpəˈnəʊvə/	n.	(天文) 超新星
surplus	/ˈsɜːpləs/	n.	剩余额;顺差;盈余
susceptible	/səˈseptəbl/	adj.	易受影响的
sustainable	/səˈsteɪnəbl/	adj.	可持续的
sympathy	/ˈsɪmpəθi/	n.	同情
synergistically	/ˌsɪnəˈdʒɪstɪkəli/	adv.	协同作用地
sanitation system			卫生系统
soft robotic			软机器人技术(指机器人在形态、功能上对人体的模拟)
stamp duty surcharge			印花税票

T

tag	/tæɡ/	n.	芯片,标签
tendon	/ˈtendən/	n.	筋,腱
tic	/tɪk/	n.	不随意的、突然发生的、快速的、反复出现的、无明显目的的、非节律性的运动或发声
toddler	/ˈtɒdlə(r)/	n.	学步的幼儿
trauma	/ˈtrɔːmə/	n.	创伤
trigger	/ˈtrɪɡə(r)/	n.	起因,诱因
tank tread			坦克履带
telescoping tube			伸缩管
The Last Judgment			《末日审判》(画)
transitional zero emission vehicles (TZEVs)			过渡性零排放车辆

Glossary

trickle-down effect			涓滴效应

U

unaccustomed	/ˌʌnəˈkʌstəmd/	adj.	不习惯的
unadvisable	/ˌʌnədˈvaɪzəbl/	adj.	不妥当的
unambiguous	/ˌʌnæmˈbɪgjuəs/	adj.	不含糊的，清楚的
unveil	/ˌʌnˈveɪl/	vt.	使公之于众
unmoored musings			天马行空

V

vagueness	/ˈveɪgnɪs/	n.	含糊，不清楚
valve	/vælv/	n.	阀，真空管
Vatican	/ˈvætɪkən/	n.	梵蒂冈
vertical	/ˈvɜːtɪkl/	adj.	垂直的，竖立的
virtual	/ˈvɜːtʃuəl/	adj.	虚拟的
visionary	/ˈvɪʒənri/	n.	有远见的人，有智慧的人
vibrating warning system			振动警报系统
Villa Savoye		n.	萨伏伊别墅
Virgin Mary		n.	圣母玛利亚（耶稣基督之母）
volatile organic compounds (VOCs)			挥发性有机物

W

wipe	/waɪp/	v.	消除，抹去（计算机、磁带或录像带上的信息等）
withdrawal	/wɪðˈdrɔːəl/	n.	移开；撤回，撤退
well-differentiated		adj.	分化良好的